Throug

JETTE FINN

Rye Bread
BOOKS

Published in 2021 by Rye Bread Books

Copyright © Jette Finn 2021

Jette Finn has asserted her right to be identified
as the author of this Work

ISBN Paperback: 979-8-9853408-0-8
Ebook: 979-8-9853408-1-5

This book is a memoir and an expression of my memories. I have
attempted to portray the truth as seen Through My Eyes and may have
modified some of the details in presenting these recollections. In the
end, my intent is to avoid causing harm to anyone.

A CIP catalogue copy of this book can be found
in the Library of Congress.

Published with the help of Indie Authors World
www.indieauthorsworld.com

IndieAuthors
World

My memoir is dedicated to my two beautiful boys
Oliver and Charlie

And to my dad whose first name was Finn which my parents
gave me as my middle name. He would have been proud to
know that I have used my name Jette Finn as the
author name of my first book 'Through My Eyes'

About the Author

Imagine sitting across the table with Jette in Cafe Luna. She is wearing her beloved old hat with bird feathers around the brim, and her green eyes are shining with enthusiasm as she shares her love for this beautiful spot in Colorado where she lives with her husband James.

Jette shows you the latest photos from her walks in the breathtaking nature here. Old Elm trees, sunflowers, silent lakes and the colorful fairy house she loves to imagine stories about whenever she walks by. "All of this might grow into new books of poetry and stories in the future," she says with a secretive smile and sips her coffee.

When you ask Jette about why she ended up here of all places, she starts telling you the tale of her life journey. From growing up in a tiny village in Denmark, to becoming an au pair in London and marrying a musician who later found fame. Then living with the glamour and shadows of the music world for decades until her marriage crumbled, and left her with her two boys to reimagine her life, starting with healing her heart and finding the way back to wholeness. A journey weaved together by wonder - with threads of resilience and self love. "This is the journey the book *Through My Eyes* is all about," she says.

Jette's eyes are deep and wise, yet she laughs like a young girl and sometimes her voice cracks with tenderness. And she leans forward and asks you about your life story and what brings you alive.

At some point your coffee cups are empty and Jette hugs you goodbye - it's time to go for her daily walk, call to catch up with her sons and little granddaughter Sophie on the other side of the world. And then enjoy writing by her desk to seize the magic of the day.

Follow Jette here:

www.facebook.com/Jette-Finn-108360298342292:

Chapter 1

The Red Tunnel

I was born in a little town called Stubbekøbing on the south coast of the island of Falster in Denmark. My entrance into this world wasn't a very celebratory moment. I recall my mother telling me that giving birth to me wasn't a memory she wanted to recall.

I was delivered at home in a room full of darkness with a gloomy light shining from above into my mother's fearful eyes, the doctor arriving only moments before I was born. He had been drinking and was breathing heavily into my mother's face, smelling of alcohol. His red silk tie was dangling over my mother's stomach as she went in and out of contractions. Each time another contraction came along, he told her to 'push harder, push harder'.

My father was nowhere to be seen; only in the distance you could hear him shouting that he couldn't cope listening to my mother's outcries of pain. So he left the house and didn't come back until the next day to see his little new bundle, the beautiful girl he had been a part of creating.

When I was ready for my journey through the never-ending tunnel of red walls through my mother's womb and seeing the light on the outside world, in my first moment of being me, I wasn't breathing. I was held upside down by the doctor under cold running water in the old sink in the very gloomy kitchen. He was holding my two sweet little feet together, which looked like an old woman's feet ready to unfold into the soft skin of youth to walk thousands of miles on the never-ending road.

There was a very bright neon light in the ceiling shining into my deep green eyes, and at the first shock of cold water touching my skin, I took my first breath of life and gave my first outcry into the world, of an unknown journey ahead of me.

Jealous Dad

My first childhood memory was when I was close to three years old, watching my father packing his suitcase while he was looking at my beautiful little face that just wanted to be loved. He said to me, 'Your mother wants me to leave.' Then he hugged me and said his goodbyes. After that I only saw him on my holidays and he married soon after leaving us, having three more children with his new wife Inga, strangely the same name as my mother.

My mother told me that my dad had kicked her in her stomach while she was nine months pregnant with me, and he was a heavy drinker and a very jealous man. I can only remember throughout my time with my dad that he was very loving towards me. Sadly, his second marriage fell apart many years later because of his drinking.

My Grandmother's Bosom

Memories are flooding back from my time as a little girl at my dad's mother's house on the island of Fyn, where she lived in a town called Svenborg. My grandfather on my dad's side died before I was born, having been an alcoholic most of his life.

My dad would take me to my grandmother's house on holidays and I was always so excited to walk up the stairs to her house holding my dad's hand. He had very big hands and my small hand seem to vanish into the palm of his, and I remember feeling safe, contented and warm with love. I knew when my grandmother opened the door that she would embrace me with her big bust pressing against my happy little face. Her beautiful Italian vintage Bucherer gold watch pendant hung over her big chest on a beautiful long gold chain, and I would look up towards her face with fascination at her big purple nose from drinking too many glasses of sweet Spanish dessert sherry wine. She told me she would buy it on her travels to the Province of Cadiz in the south of Spain where the sherry was made of Pedro and Moscatel blended grapes.

I would put my arms around her but could only reach halfway around her big waist. Her bust would feel warm against my face and very soothing, and her head would bend down, looking at me. Her long hair was tightly curled and upswept into a poof on top of her head; it was a bit shorter at the sides, with curls. I was mesmerised by her hair and wondered how long it took her every morning to put it up. Did she put her lemon-coloured vintage Sicilian dress on first before doing her hair?

She told me to sit up straight in her soft, dusty green velvet dining chair, which she had told me was a sixteenth century Italian antique. I had been bending down to look underneath the hand-carved mahogany Benetti table, fascinated by her feet covered in her vintage emerald-green Italian silk pumps. I was so excited to know we were having afternoon tea in her beautiful Italian Ginori porcelain cups. They had this vibrant green and gold line along the rim, and I would stir my Earl Grey tea scented with lemon balm with a vintage Italian silver teaspoon, which always seem to make the tea taste better. The lemon would float on the top and I could see this beautiful pattern of snowflakes looking like stars smiling at me. The tablecloth was bought in Italy on one of my grandmother's many journeys travelling to the north of Tuscany and Venice. It was made of soft white linen, and I would count all the hand-sewn lavender flowers along the edges, imagining they would come to life and fall into a vase, spreading their fragrance over the table while we were sitting sipping the tea.

Mermaid Maybelline

I fell into my dreams with excitement, knowing that we would be going on my uncle's ship the next morning. I happily jumped into bed with my soft mermaid rag doll with orange hair, her fishtail glowing fluorescent green. I named her Maybelline which means lovable, and she was in the story of my favourite book, *The Little Mermaid* written by the Danish author Hans Christian Andersen. I loved the story, and the author was born in Odense, the town next to Svenborg where my grandmother lived. I fell asleep in my grandmother's antique Italian maplewood bed with the most beautiful silk duvet over me in a shade of blue, covered in a pattern of multicoloured shells. In my dreams Maybelline and I would be swimming through a tunnel of blue water up to the surface, Maybelline would turn her fishtail into long slender legs and I would turn into a princess, and we would fly together up into the stars for the night with my H C Andersen book under my arm.

My Uncle's Ship

The morning came and I put Maybelline and my book under my pillow for my return that night after my journey on my uncle's ship. He was the captain of the ship sailing across the sea from Fyn to the other island of Als. He was a tall man with a long beard, and he had a nice smile with very white teeth. He put his captain's hat on my head, and he put me up on a high stool and said to me, 'You sail the ship.' I put my little hands on the steering wheel, and I felt this excitement of being in control of it. I felt my uncle's big hands on top of mine and he told me, 'We are zig-zagging now as it allows us to turn the bow towards the wind, as it changes from one side to the other.'

We were gliding through the water and my little fingers were holding on so tight to the wheel that my hands were starting to feel numb, but it didn't matter as I felt I had gone to heaven sailing this big ship with my uncle. My face felt windswept, and I had very red cheeks which were glowing in the dark when we returned to shore, and we went back to my uncle's house for dinner which was a feast itself.

Fields of Gold

I could hear my aunt in the kitchen talking to my dad and the aroma of the roast in the oven was filling the dining room with a wonderful smell which made me feel very hungry. I sat myself at the dining table which was decorated with a white linen tablecloth and my aunt's best white dining plates with little hand-painted violets around the edges. The table was beautifully laid, and the wine glasses were shaped like a woman's body; they had a little gold line around the rim of the glass with gold stars falling over the glass on one side. It was a magical table filled with beauty, and my dad put a vase in the middle filled with wildflowers I had picked from my aunt's garden.

I felt I was in a fairy tale wonderland as I daydreamed of sitting in the fields of wildflowers, sipping a little wine as the twinkling gold stars flew off the glass and danced in the sunlight around the glass. I was dressed in a floaty blue and white cotton vintage dress with fluttery sleeves which my grandmother had bought me in Italy, and I was dreaming of dancing with the gold stars, feeling the wet grass under my bare feet.

I fell out of my dreams when my aunt told me to sit up straight and asked me, 'Why have you been laying your head on the table and moving the glasses around?'

I told her, 'I have been in fields of gold, dancing with the stars.' She shook her head at me, and I put the glasses back next to the plates while she was putting the roast on the table. We all sat down to a feast of beautiful food, talking of what adventures tomorrow would bring.

I listened to the humming of people's voices around the magical dining table which made me sleepy, and, my dad carried me into bed and I put on my pajamas my grandmother had bought me in Italy. They were made of cotton in a pale blue colour with a design of red roses. I pulled out Maybelline and my book which was still under my pillow, and I put them close to me while my dad covered me up with the dreamy silk duvet and kissed my cheeks and I fell into my dreams of another exciting day tomorrow.

Chapter 2

Neon Lights

I would often have nightmares of leaving my grandmother's house, having felt loved and cared for, and then saying our goodbyes as my dad and I took the train across the island from Svendborg to the island of Sjaelland. We would get off the train at Copenhagen's central station, where I would end my holidays at my dad's house. Memories are flowing back to me of being frightened of sleeping in the living room and seeing the neon advertisement lights flashing through the window, and I would hide underneath the heavy, cold, damp duvet while I could hear my dad in the kitchen drinking one beer after another. . . he was a serious alcoholic by then.

His wife, Inga, would take me to the movies to get away from my dad. We would get on an old bus which would rumble along, the movement of the bus making Inga's stomach move from side to side. It felt warm when I put my little hands on it. It was the shape of a round football, as she was heavily pregnant with their third child.

I could feel the baby kicking and my fingers would move around, playing with the baby's feet through the delicate skin.

Inga had a baby-pink woollen headscarf over her long brown hair, tied in a knot under her chin, and I would lean my head against her chest which was covered with an old creamy mint-coloured wool cardigan which was full of holes and was itching my face. But I didn't mind as the comfort of being close to her made me feel safe and I would end up dozing off in her lap with the sound and the rumbling movements of the bus.

I opened my eyes when she called my name saying, 'We have to get off the bus now,' and I looked at her brown woven leather low-heeled vintage shoes which had seen better days. She had swollen ankles as she had water retention in her body because of the baby.

I was wearing an old dark blue woollen Paddington Bear coat with a hood. It was a little too small for me and the buttons wouldn't do up, so she took off her woollen headscarf and put it around my neck as it was a very cold night. We would hold hands and get off the bus and head to the movie theatre.

I was looking forward to sitting down next to her and holding her hand, eating popcorn with the other hand while we watched *The Wizard of Oz* with Judy Garland. After the movie was finished, we would get on the bus and go home after hours in Kansas, living in Dorothy's world.

The Ruby Slippers

My dad would be lying on the couch fast asleep after drinking too much. Inga would light a cigarette and sit herself down on the old brown wicker chair with her feet up on the vintage orange leather Hamden footstool which she had found in a secondhand shop downtown. Her swollen ankles seemed to go down as she leaned her head against the back of the chair, and I would crawl into their bed, falling asleep still in my Paddington coat and with Maybelline in my arms. I dropped my book *The Little Mermaid* on the floor as I fell into my dreams of being Dorothy wearing the ruby red slippers and holding the little dog, Toto, in my arms, and we would be sucked into the tornado and fly over the rainbow, way up high.

Bakken

Many years later, after his second divorce, my dad decided to move to a home for the elderly and even though he had been clean of alcohol for fifteen years, his body and mind had been damaged over the years.

I can still feel to this day the warmth of him hugging me in his room where the walls were covered with pictures of his four children, and we would talk of good times. We talked of the day many moons ago when we walked hand in hand in the forest close to a fairground called Bakken, which is the oldest amusement park in the world, located in the outskirts of Copenhagen. I was only six years old, and we sat ourselves down on a log to have ice cream. I loved strawberry flavour, with another scoop of vanilla on top in a cone, and there was a spoonful of jam right at the top running down the sides. I had to lick fast as a few drops of the jam would drip onto my navy-blue dress. There were little rosebuds sewn onto the sleeves by my grandmother to make the dress look special.

I had little short white socks on and sparkly flat silver shoes with ankle straps. We started to walk towards Bakken, enjoying our ice creams, when suddenly a horse which had escaped the carriage it was supposed to be drawing, came galloping towards us. My dad threw me into a ditch in the grass which was full of stinging nettles and my ice cream flew up in the air and landed on a tree, looking like a Christmas decoration.

My dad jumped into the ditch too and protected me, embracing me in his arms, and saved me from the horse kicking me as it passed very close to us. My legs were in so much pain after being covered in stinging nettles, my dad spat on a white silk handkerchief he had in the little top pocket of his black jacket, to dab on my skin as it calmed down the pain on my legs. He lifted me up and carried me the rest of the way into Bakken and it was so comforting, feeling his warm breath against my cheeks, as it didn't smell of alcohol but sweet ice cream, and he had a little jam at the corner of his lips which made his smile look bigger to me.

Shadows on the Wall

While we were sitting on his bed in his room talking of all these moments we have had together, just me and my dad, he started to make little shadow animals on the wall with his hands against the light of the lamp. It looked like a camel to me and sometimes a deer. He said to me, 'Do you remember I used to tell you stories of these shadows on the wall as bedtime stories?' I said I did, as he was an amazing storyteller and he could have written children's books. My dad was a very spiritual soul, but life just got in the way for him to be creative.

As we sat there on his bed talking, I asked him, 'What can you remember of your childhood? We have never spoken about that.' He turned to me with tears in his eyes, and said, 'It was a very hard upbringing; as you know my father died when I was three years old. My mother brought me and my two brothers up on her own. My mother always relied on me as I was the oldest of her children, and in many ways my life has been about pleasing her and not much about what my life could have been.'

I hugged him and said, 'Perhaps your drinking from an early age was one of the results of the traumatic times throughout your life, not knowing who you were as your loving self?'

'Yes, I think you're right,' he said.

I hugged him again even closer and said, 'I'm so happy you are sharing this with me so I can understand where you are coming from, and I will treasure that in my heart, Dad.'

We hugged a little more, still sitting on his bed. He was wearing a deep red woollen vintage robe I had bought him the Christmas before. The colour red symbolises passion and energy, which my dad was so much lacking in, but he looked so handsome in the dressing gown with his beautiful brown eyes and a head full of grey hair which hung down over his eyes like Elvis Presley's. It made him look so full of life and he told me he loved me and was sorry for all the years we had lost along the way, not seeing each other.

I moved a bit of his hair to the side and kissed him on the forehead and felt my tears running down over his face, which I wiped off with his white silk handkerchief.

He laid himself down on the bed saying to me, 'I would like you to have my silk handkerchief.' I put it in the little pocket I had on the front of my ocean-blue shirt, feeling it close to my heart. He closed his eyes as he didn't like watching me leaving and saying my goodbyes as I was flying back to England that evening.

I never saw my dad again. He died that winter from an ulcer. He was eighty-three years old. . .

Chapter 3

The Cherry Tree

My dearest grandmother on my mother's side lived across the road from my parents' house, when we lived on the south coast of Denmark on the island of Falster in a small, very quiet village called Blaesbjerg. My grandmother would be my saviour if I had been sitting daydreaming in the birch trees in front of her house, listening to the wind blowing through the trees, the little heart-shaped leaves sounding like little gold pennies making music.

It was a gorgeous place to sit and daydream, forgetting time, a habit which has followed me through life.

My grandmother's youngest child, Anne, was seventeen when I was nine years old, and she was my idol of beauty. My grandmother would put hot water into the old lemon-coloured crackle-glazed bowl for my aunt to wash herself (they didn't have a shower or bathroom). I would be sitting on an old cushion, covered in a strawberry colour red silk on the creaky old mustard-yellow wicker chair, watching my aunt washing herself. My grandmother had sewn the cushion on her hand sewing machine with the pedal underneath, tapping her foot up and down which always was a soothing sound to me.

The old chair was standing in the kitchen against the window between the sewing table on the left and the dining table on the right. From the window you had a view of the garden where I would sit in the old cherry tree in the summertime, eating the most beautiful black cherries and ending up with a stomachache.

My grandmother would look at me and say, 'Have you been eating my cherries?' I would look at her with an innocent smile and was told to stick my tongue out which would be purple from the juice. She always smiled at me and said I looked pretty with the juices down my chin. My white T-shirt underneath my pale blue dungarees would not be white any more, and my bare feet had a pattern of juice running between my toes, looking to me like purple morning glory flowers.

Lace Ribbons

I came out of my daydreaming, still watching my aunt washing her beautiful curvy body in little stages of pulling her dandelion-colour cotton nightie with lace ribbons on it, halfway down to her waist, washing her breasts and under her arms with a soft lavender-blue flannel. The soap she was washing herself with had a scent of jasmine and it filled the kitchen with the smells of warm summer days.

She would put her long blonde hair up with one of my grandmother's hand-painted hair combs which still smelled of my grandmother's very fine hair. Mesmerised by her beauty, as she was washing her face and around her neckline, I would fall back into my dreams of watching my grandmother putting her combs in her hair on early rising. She had a special way of putting them in her hair. She would lift her hair high up with the comb and then push it down a little towards her face on either side with her crooked, worn-out fingers, which had a story of their own to tell.

The old crackled-glazed bowl was also used to make bread dough. My grandmother would put the bowl with the dough in it to rise under the duvet on her bed, and I would crawl underneath to watch it rise. The bread would come out of the oven smelling sweet after it was baked, and she would cut a thick slice for me and put a thick spread of butter on it with a heavenly, tasty, homemade raspberry jam. The first bite always made my mouth water.

Birch Tree Dreams

I would often sit in my grandmother's birch trees, imagining the branches were shaped like little Hobbits with long ears and big feet, and the golden leaves would shine on their feet before falling to the ground. My Aunt Anne would often stand underneath the birch trees kissing her boyfriend goodbye. I would sit quietly watching them kissing from the branches above and I dreamed of a romance with a prince on a white horse coming to rescue me – which nearly became a reality later in my adulthood.

My grandmother's voice got my attention; it was time to go home. I would jump down to the ground and fall into her arms, and she would take my hand and walk me back to my house knowing that there would be trouble with my mother as I had forgotten the time.

The Chocolate Box

On that particular day as my grandmother handed me over to my mother, she told her to be nice to me as I hadn't done anything wrong. My mother was pregnant with my sister then, and I was nine years old. I ran into my room and found an old chocolate box my grandmother had given me to celebrate when my two little front milk teeth had fallen out. It had been full of delicious milk chocolates with colourful wrappers which I had folded nicely into a little pile and left in the box after I had eaten the chocolates with great delight.

The aroma of the chocolates was still lingering in the box, and I had been keeping my little dried red rose petals in it which I had collected in the garden and the box had become very precious to me. My mother called me into her room, and I brought my box with me to give it to her, hoping it would help me to lessen the guilt of sitting daydreaming on top of the world in my grandmother's trees.

She took the box out of my hand and threw it up in the air, and all the red rose petals flew up towards the ceiling in slow motion. I grabbed the box, trying to save the rose petals as they were falling, filling up my chocolate box again.

She shouted at me as I left the room, 'The smell of chocolate makes me feel nauseous! Go back to your room!'

'But I just want to be with you and cuddle your round stomach and feel my baby sister kicking,' I told her. She turned over on her side with great difficulty and ignored my plea to be close to her.

I left the room feeling sad and laid myself down on my bed, wrapping myself into the patchwork bedspread my grandmother had made me and fell into a dream to the sound of her sewing machine watching her delicate hands sewing those beautiful dresses for her daughters. I found myself in one of her beautiful creations. I would dance across the dance floor with no inhibitions, not caring where I was, and feeling the music in my body as my young feet, in light-blue ballerina shoes, were sliding across the room with not a care in the world. I fell into a deep sleep with much sadness thinking of my chocolate box.

Chapter 4

The Magic Box

Many times, I would walk down to the sea with my friends who lived in the same village as me. I would be wearing my sky-blue jeans shorts and a baby-green T-shirt, and a pair of baby-blue linen canvas lace-up boots.

I would take my boots off and tie the vibrant bright lime-coloured laces together into a knot and hang them over my shoulders, and we would walk hand in hand onto the beach, feeling the warm sand between our toes. We would count the vibrant rainbow-coloured seashells covered in sand and pick them up and put them into our pockets. The sand would fall through the holes in our pockets, leaving a trail behind us as we made our way back to my grandmother's house.

I would keep my seashells in the magic box made of mother-of-pearl which my grandmother's mother had given her when she was a little girl. She would keep the magic box in the loft bedroom, where I would sleep heavily without a worry in the world, contentedly knowing that all my little seashells were safely hidden in a good place. I would some-times take them out and put them into my grandmother's bed and cover them with the very heavy duvet, and they would shine in the dark and I would imagine the smell of the sea where I had walked in the sand, feeling the hardness of the seashells hurting my feet, but calling to me to pick them up.

I loved sleeping in my grandmother's house. It was blissful just being there late evenings, listening to my grandparents talking and playing cards at the mahogany dining table, always shining brightly from my grandmother's polishing. The late sunset light would be beaming through the window, and it made all these shadows of dancing fingers playing the colourful Queens and Kings in the middle of the table, and the silence of the concentration of who would win the hand was exhilarating to me.

The Hot Brick

The fireplace would be alight, and the crackling of the fire soothed me. I was excited to have a sleepover as my grandmother would heat up a brick by the fireplace to put in the bed, and a blanket to put on top of the damp duvet. The loft room was freezing, and we would climb the steep staircase with very narrow, worn-out steps from many years of my grandmother climbing them with her seven children who used to sleep in the loft rooms.

I would jump into bed where my grandmother had put the hot brick down at the end of the bed, and it was heavenly to put your cold feet on it and cover yourself up with the warm blanket too.

The Swallow's Nest

After the card game was over, my grandmother would make hot chocolate in the kitchen on the old Aga cast iron stove, removing the cast iron rings one by one and putting some more wood down inside of it which she had cut into small logs on early rising. The Aga was on all day heating up the house, and the smell of the wood clung to my grandmother's apron.

I would watch her making hot chocolate while I was listening to the swallows who had a nest in the outdoor toilet. They would come back every spring and I loved sitting in the toilet watching them flying in and out, building their nests. They somehow became my friends, and I was daydreaming of flying away with them to the warm countries I didn't know I would be travelling to in my adulthood.

CHAPTER 5

The Glass Bowl of Sweets

I loved watching my grandmother getting dressed in the mornings. She wore stockings held up by shiny little pink cotton buttons, and she would always have to rearrange them through the day as they seemed to fall down through her daily chores. The sounds of her thick dark brown stockings were somehow very comforting to me as her thighs rubbed together when she walked across the floor in her old worn-out leather slippers. The sound of her opening a little cabinet in the back kitchen area was a joyous ringing of a bell hanging on the doorknob on a silk ribbon, and the smell of sweets she had in a little glass bowl with hand-painted red roses on it was, for me, the most exciting moment. She would tell me to hold up my warm little hands tightly together, and she would lift the glass bowl to my hands, and the sweets wrapped in different coloured paper would dance into the palms of my hands. I would close my hands together and sit by the kitchen window counting how many I was lucky enough to get.

I looked at all the beautiful, framed photos of the family filling up a whole wall, filled with the history of her children born at home and brought up in the house my grandad had built where he and my grandmother had lived all their lives. I would put the little sweets in a wooden bowl my dad had made when he was a little boy. I painted it algae green with a little bluebell flower on top of the lid, and it followed me through life to many places on my travels.

Gold Teeth

My grandfather used to have a nap in the afternoons in the living room. The old dusty couch faced the garden window which was covered by a white climbing rose whose fragrance was overpowering as it danced through the room. I watched him sleeping with his mouth wide open and listened to his heavy breathing while I sat on the old rocking chair, and I felt mesmerised by his two gold teeth right at the front of his mouth, reflecting the sunbeams coming through the window.

His feet hung out over the end of the couch, and I knew when he started to rub his thick socks against each other that he was waking up slowly. He would rub his eyes and he knew I was sitting in the rocking chair, patiently waiting for him to wake up.

Sugar Cubes

He took my hand, and we sat down in the back kitchen, on the old bench against the wall which was covered with colourful puffed-up cushions that my grandmother had sewn on her hand sewing machine out of old material from her children's clothing. I sat next to him waiting for the hot coffee my grandmother had made in an old blue enamel coffee pot. I loved that coffee pot as my grandad had painted blueberries on it with little green leaves around the edges. My grandad dipped the sugar cubes into the hot coffee, and he looked at me. I opened my mouth with great enjoyment as the sugar cube melted in my mouth.

The sound of my grandmother standing scratching her back against a corner of the kitchen door, wearing her worn-out old cotton dress with the apron still wrapped around her waist. Her big breasts which had fed seven children over the years, moved from side to side while we were having a chat with my mouth full of sugar cubes.

The afternoon passed quickly, and my grandmother would put her red scarf on her head as she didn't like the wind blowing into her ears, then I knew it was time for her to walk me home across the fields back to my mother and my stepfather.

CHAPTER 6

Tinkerbell

My mother married my stepdad not long after her first marriage with my dad ended. My stepdad often asked me through my teenage life, 'When are you moving out?' My mother never seemed to hear his words, or perhaps she just ignored them. And that was the beginning of the end of my dream world of hoping to be in my mother's loving arms forever. As time went by, she became more and more distant, and ignored my stepdad's behaviour towards me throughout my youth. Her love for me was only in my dreamer's imagination of hoping that one day she would hold and hug me again.

One of my fearful memories as a little girl was when I was locked into our living room while my mother and stepdad went out to town. I still remember the wallpaper. It was light purple with lilac flowers on it.

I would imagine sitting by the window waiting for my little fairy friend, Tinkerbell, from the movie *Peter Pan*. She would fly up to the window with her little wings full of twinkling lights around her, and I would open the window, letting her into my lonely childhood world. She would use her magic wand, and I would have wings for the night.

We would fly away together into the warm air, with the stars twinkling in the sky as two little fairies looking for a place where people would welcome us into their homes and give us shelter for the night. As I was imagining all these fantasies in my mind, I would lay myself down on our big old couch which was covered in dark blue velvet fabric, and I would crunch myself into a little snowball and cover myself in an old blanket which I can still remember the musty smell of. The dampness in the dark room felt haunting and I would close my eyes hoping that my parents would be coming home soon. . .

My Mother's Heartbeat

I do remember times when I would love being with my mother and my stepdad.

We drove on my stepdad's motorbike through pouring rain to his mum and dad's house. I was five years old, and I was wearing my very soft white fur coat, a matching hat with hand-sewn flowers around the rim, and matching white woolly tights with white American Peek-a Boo wellie boots. I loved my wellies as, ever since I was a little girl, I had dreamed of one day travelling to America and being a cowgirl. It kind of became real much later in my life.

I felt very comfortable driving along on the bike, sitting between my stepdad and my mother; she would put her arms around me, and I would put my arms around my stepdad. I felt my mother's heartbeat against me and the warmth of my step-dad's back, covered in a big brown leather coat he managed to get during the short time he was conscripted into the army.

He used to tell stories of the things he got up to and was told to do in the army. If he was told to march forward, he would march backwards and sit himself in a tree and stay there until he was told to get down. Then they put him into the hospital saying he was not fit to be in the army, and he got away with it.

I would still be sitting on the motorbike feeling warm but a little wet as the rain came down fast. My little curls underneath my fur hat that my mother had curled with a tong earlier that day were now hanging straight down over my fur coat.

Baby Doll Carriage Pram

We arrived at my stepdad's parents' house, and they were a very eccentric couple. I would be in another world there. I was entertained by my stepdad's sister who had a black cat called Oscar with a cute little white nose. She would dress him up in baby clothes and put him in a baby doll carriage pram which she had sat in herself when she was a little girl. We would walk the pram down the lane to the playground where there was a swing I loved to go on. I swung too high and fell off the swing and had to go to the hospital to have a few stitches in my forehead. I always think of that moment in time when I touch the little scar on the left of my forehead close to my hairline.

I was amazed by my stepdad's mother's hand-knitted slippers. She had sewn a leather sole on them, but somehow as the years went by, the sole would end up on top of the slipper, so it began to look like a pair of leather slippers with a knitted sole. She never told me how that happened and I'm not sure if she ever realised what she was walking on. She had a lovely voice and often sat by the dining table by the old vintage red and blue cottage tablecloth. It never came off but was only folded half to one side, and folded out again when it was time to eat. She used to sing 'Any Woman's Blues' by Ida Cox and Mamie Smith songs like 'Crazy Blues'. I loved sitting there by the kitchen table, mesmerised by her slippers and listening to her beautiful voice filling the room with calmness. Even the mad cat, Oscar, stopped scratching at the walls where he would make long claw marks down the wall, which never seemed to bother anyone and started to look like an abstract wallpaper.

A 1950's Packard Bell TV was sitting on a very high shelf and we all had neck pain after watching a movie for two hours looking up all the time. My stepdad's dad would sit on a high chair right in front of the TV so we couldn't see much from the musty old couch behind him. It had big holes in the upholstery, which was always covered over with some funky old cloth which always fell down behind you and you had to pull it up again.

The Empty Sardine Cans

I loved going up the stairs to my stepdad's dad's bedroom. He collected empty sardine cans lined up on a table and I would fall into my dreams, imagining it was New York City as I had seen it in old Hollywood movies with their tall buildings and yellow taxis. I pictured the Statue of Liberty on Liberty Island, which is made of cast iron and stainless steel on the inside, and on the outside is made of copper, all the way from ground level to torch, and also The Empire State Building, a 102-storey art deco skyscraper in midtown Manhattan. I didn't know that I would walk up the stairs of the torch of the Statue of Liberty many years later and take the lift to the 102-story floor of the Empire State with my son Oliver when he was a little boy.

I never found out why my stepdad's dad collected sardine cans, but I loved sitting in his room building New York out of sardine cans.

I was fascinated by his very big woolly pyjamas which hung on a big nail on the back of his bedroom door. Most of his clothes hung on nails hammered onto the walls. I thought it looked very decorative and colourful. I loved being in their house as we had a lot of fun, and often we all sang old blues songs together as I sat on his mother's warm lap wrapped in her arms, looking down at her old brown worn out tights which somehow ended up in her hand-knitted slippers. She smelled of the old 1940's perfume *L'Air du Temps* by Nina Ricci which I would sell many years later in my second job being a sales girl in a clothing shop when I was eighteen; I always thought about her when I put a little dab behind my ears, remembering sitting on her lap singing the blues.

Oscar

There was a teak Danish chest standing against the wall in the living room with drawers half open, as you could never close them properly. The top drawer was full of colourful yarn, and you would just pull out the colour you needed if you wanted to knit or sew something. The cat, Oscar, would often jump into the drawer and get its claws caught in the yarn and then make spiders' webs out of the yarn, crossing the room from wall to wall, and you had to try and fight your way through it when you walked through the room.

It was a house where I would love to dream time away and it all became magical to me, and I never wanted to go home.

The Magical Scooter

Sometimes they would travel as a family to our house not far from where they lived. The mother would take the bus and the father would get on his old retro Italian-style black chrome-plated moped, and my stepdad's sister would hang on behind on her white roller skates which had rubber wheels on them. I would sit in the living room by the window at our house waiting for them to arrive, as I knew the father would take me on his scooter letting me sit on his lap, and we would drive around the neighbourhood. It was magical, as I felt I was steering the scooter and there was something exhilarating and fun about the speed we were going. Little did I know that many years later I would be on a Harley Davidson with a friend, driving down those winding roads in North Carolina.

CHAPTER 7

The Christmas Dance

I knew that I was an accident and not the result of the mirac-
ulous journey of a child being made of two people who had
fallen in love before I came into this world, and I have very few
memories of being loved.

Though I did have loving moments with my mother. I loved
her beauty and her sense of fashion. She would dress in high-
waisted black cigarette-leg jeans and a white, tie-neck, short-
sleeved blouse cropped at the waist, with flat black pointed-toe
shoes made of Napa leather.

She dressed me in a little girl's Cinderella-style full circle tea
dress, collared with lace and with hand-embroidered red roses
at the yoke of the dress. It's the only dress I have kept, with
memories of my mother when we went to a Christmas dance
where my grandfather was playing in a little band. He was
playing his violin he had bought in Germany and which I
inherited, and it now has a home here in my house. It has travelled all the way from Denmark to England and now America
where I live today. . .

I remember dancing with my mother around the Christmas tree, holding her delicate hands which felt very comforting and safe, and she would kiss me on my very warm cheeks and my hair hanging over my shoulders felt wet from the sweat on my neck. My mother would gently wipe my neck with a rose-printed handkerchief her mother gave her to try and cool me down. I never wanted to wash those kisses away on my cheeks as they made me feel wanted.

The Bunny Rabbit

I remember moments together with my mother when I was ten years old. I had a colouring book where there was a drawing of a little soft-coated white bunny rabbit with big, long ears and a short puffy tail. My mother coloured it white but she thought the tail was a flower and she coloured it cherry red.

We giggled so hard that my stomach hurt, and we held each other tight, and I didn't want to let go of my mother's arms. I imagined the bunny rabbit jumping out of the painting and landing on my lap. Me and my mother would stroke its soft coat and it would be tapping its teeth lightly together and would communicate with its body language and its little noises. We giggled some more, apologising for colouring its tail red. It would jump back into the colouring book and my mother would try to paint its little fluffy tail white, but it became pink instead. I still have the colouring book, and sometimes I get it out and wonder why my mother found it so difficult to love me.

Knitting Needles

She would also knit little dresses for my teenage doll, and I used to sit close to her on the old almond-coloured couch in the living room. I could feel the knitting needles against my arm going from side to side and it felt soothing, and we had something to share after the dress was finished. It was made of a golden yellow wool yarn and there was a gathering at the waist where my mother had crocheted a long string to tie around the dress. I would put the dress on the teenage doll which had very long slender legs.

I thought she looked beautiful, and I would dance with her in the living room and my mother would join in.

The Chocolate Moustache

We would have days where she would tell me to take the day off school and we would go to a big store in Copenhagen called Magasin, where we would sit in their restaurant and drink hot chocolate which had a big blob of whipped cream on top. I would have a moustache on my top lip from the cream and my mother would wipe it clean with her handkerchief which smelled of her perfume. We would share a big piece of chocolate sponge cake filled with cream and jam. I loved those moments of her being loving to me.

As I got older, these moments of joy became rare as she became more and more jealous of me being young while she was getting older.

My Grandmother's Bedspread

On my eighteenth birthday, I was having a party in a dance hall where I lived, in the town Naerum, north of Copenhagen. I had invited all my school friends and was very excited seeing them all that night. I was picking blue anemones in the forest where I lived as they are in season in April and they indicate spring time. The Danish poet Kaj Munk, killed by the Gestapo in 1944 wrote, a touching poem called 'The Blue Anemone'. I would make little bouquets of them and put them in vases which were hand-painted with green leaves along one side. The white cotton tablecloths looked lovely on the tables with the lavender-scented candles and the vases with the blue anemones on each one. It was a setting I had lovingly put together for my party, with the room smelling of the soft, powdery but pungent scent of the anemones, and I was looking forward for the party to begin.

The evening came around and I was stressed out about what to wear, and my mother kindly let me wear one of her dresses for the evening. It was a hand-sewn, Seventies-style, long-sleeved, floral maxi dress, and I had low-heel red pumps to go with the dress. My hair hanging over my shoulders flicked away from the sides, and I felt like a million dollars.

The party started and we danced the night away. My boyfriend, Jan, and I were dancing to the song *All Right Now* by the band Free, and suddenly my mother was standing in the room crying, saying she had thrown my stepdad out of our house and she wanted a divorce. She told me the party was over and wanted me to come home with her.

That was the end of the party I had looked forward to for so long. When we got home, my mother was still crying, and I had to comfort her and forget it was my eighteenth birthday. We hugged, and I said it was okay that my party was ruined, but she pushed me away and told me to go to bed. I laid myself down on my bed, wrapping myself into the bedspread my grandmother had made for me, and I cried myself to sleep, missing my grandmother so much, and her loving hands which were always there to hold mine if I was in trouble with my mother.

CHAPTER 8

Why Didn't You Love Me?

When I was thirty-six years old, I travelled on my own to my mother's country house in Denmark. I wanted to talk to her about why she didn't love me. When I asked her the question face to face, she ignored it and turned to my grandmother who was visiting the house. My mother said to my grandmother, 'Let's go and have a look at the flowers in the garden.'

I felt very sad that my grandmother would sit there in the middle of the room between my mother and me, as I loved my grandmother more than my own mother. I was heaving for air as I was in so much pain, wanting my mother to talk to me and tell me she loved me. I pleaded with her to sit down so we could talk, but she looked straight at me with so much anger and then turned her back and led my grandmother out to the garden.

I felt so frustrated by the need to know why she didn't want to talk to me. I wanted her to tell me of her childhood and her upbringing, and to know why she had a fear of darkness all through her life. My mother's sister, Gunver, who's my godmother, told me that she was afraid of sleeping in her own bed and they often slept in the same bed. So much I wanted to know of her childhood, and perhaps understand why she found it difficult to love me. I begged her to sit down and talk to me but she ignored me again, so I told her I was driving back to Copenhagen and would be flying back to England the next morning. Before I left the house my grandmother came to me and hugged me and said, 'I love you. Be safe.'

I drove back to Copenhagen in a daze of tears, and I called my husband who didn't seem to care much about what had happened. I spoke to our son Oliver who was four years old at the time and, said goodnight to him and I'd see him tomorrow.

The Goodbye at The Airport

The next morning came and I headed for the airport. After I checked in, I called my mother, and she answered the phone. I was feeling tearful and people were staring at me. I said to her, 'Please can we talk?' She hung up on me and we didn't talk for two years or more.

I wanted to ask my grandmother what had happened when my mother was a child: was she loved by her and my grandfather? She told me she did her best for her seven children, but that generation never talked openly of what love for one another meant to them. I remember sitting on the old chair in the middle of my grandmother's kitchen, I was wrapped in a blanket my grandmother had made for me that had always been very comforting to snuggle up to. I had to wait until my thirties to be told that when she was pregnant for the fifth time with my mother, the doctor had told her to go home and be ashamed of herself. I can't imagine how she must have felt being told that; if you fell pregnant in those days, it wasn't really a woman's choice, as you obeyed your husband's needs.

The Unkissed Lips

After my grandfather died, my grandmother became a happy soul and at last was able to shine her beauty for the next ten years. She started to wear colourful clothes and jewellery and a little makeup. I remember visiting her at the house were she was sitting on her favorite armchair watching the TV at high volume as she wasn't allowed to have it loud when my grandfather was alive. She looked beautiful in her red woollen dress, still wearing the old leather slippers. I loved the sound they made when she walked across a room; it was soothing to me. She had a necklace her mother had given to her when she was young. It was made of sea pearls, and it twinkled like little stars all over her dress, and she had put rouge on her cheeks and a red lipstick on her tender lips which hadn't been kissed for years, or maybe never.

My godmother, Gunver, her daughter, was a hairdresser and she had curled her fine hair and put it all together at the back with her old tortoiseshell hair comb. I will never forget that moment in time, seeing her feeling like a woman after a hard life living on a farm with seven children and a husband who was a bit of a dictator. I never saw her looking so beautiful.

Karen

My grandfather was an architect, and I loved watching him drawing houses. He would sometimes put me on his lap and give me the pencil he was drawing with while holding my hand and helping me to draw the lines. It was magic seeing the house appear, with his help, as if I were the artist. He also built the house I lived in with my parents just across the road from my grandparents.

There was a little sculpture of a girl made of clay standing on the corner of my grandfather's office desk. Her sunflower-coloured dress was blowing up around her waist and she had a dusty green scarf on her head. I named her Karen after my grandmother. Today she is standing on a little table close to the living room windows facing our front garden in our house here in America. She has been travelling from Denmark to England, and from England to America. Every time I look at her, I think of my grandfather sitting by his desk drawing houses and always having a cigarette burning in the ashtray. The cigarette smoke sometimes made a little cloud around Karen, and I would move her to another place in the living room, imagining that she was asking me to save her from the smoke.

My grandfather's name was Valdemar and he never played with his own children or showed any kind of love towards them. He wasn't a very tall man, as he had polio when he was a little boy and he stopped growing, and he did have a complex about being a small man through his adulthood. He died ten years before my grandmother, never feeling worthy about himself.

Housemaid

When my grandmother decided she was tired of living, she laid herself down on her bed in the fine dining room in 1995. She was eighty-six years old.

My uncle Helmer, one of her sons, was holding her hand through her last hours and they talked about all the good times of family gatherings. They were looking at old photos through my grandmother's lifetime of having seven children and a farm and a husband she didn't love. I remember she told me once that she had never loved my grandfather but was forced to marry him through her parents' wishes. When she was a young girl, she was a housemaid in someone's house, and she fell in love with the man who was taking care of the tasks at the farm. When she left her job, she never saw him again until sixty-five years later. When she met him again after my grandfather had been dead for many years, it was in a place in her hometown where older people met up for coffees. She invited him to her home, and after he had been there for a while, she asked him to leave as he was being very bossy towards her She told him she had been married to a very controlling husband for far too many years and she didn't need another man to tell her what to do. She was eighty-five at the time and it still makes me laugh, but I feel sadness that her whole life was being a housewife, having children one after the other while running a small farm. I would have wished for her to have been with someone she truly loved.

Floating Swim Fins

I remember when Uncle Helmer, who was a builder, came to my grandmother's house. I would be sitting down on my favourite old chair in the kitchen, listening to him talking to my grandmother. He never sat down; always walking backwards and forwards from wall to wall with his cigar in his mouth. His big clogs made this very comforting sound every time he took a step on the old wooden floorboards. The kitchen seemed to have his footsteps printed into the floor from walking miles backwards and forwards. Sometimes I would put my little feet into his footprints, and it was like swimming in the sea with big floating swim fins.

I loved listening to them talking about Anna next door with the chickens. She had a funny walk like a duck, as one of her legs was shorter than the other. I watched her when she came home from the village grocery shop on the corner at the end of our road, and she had a basket hanging on the front of the bicycle full of home-grown vegetables and fruit. When she saw me coming out of my grandmother's front door, she hopped off the bicycle, as she was not very tall and she had to reach up to the basket hanging on the front of the bicycle to get a treat for me. I never knew what I was going to have. It was always a surprise, but I hoped for an apple as they were so juicy, and when I took a bite, it would be dripping down my chin.

Anna's chickens always woke me up at the crack of dawn, making soft chirps. I loved listening to them when I was staying overnight at my grandmother's. They had names and I liked the hen called Rose who had a very pink comb and starry eyes. Her comb looked very elegant, and I learned later in life that the comb is considered an organ, as it controls their body temperature. Rose liked me and sometimes I played with her in Anna's garden while I would share my apple with her.

Lollipops

I walked from my grandmother's house to the ice cream house on hot summer days. It was Alice who owned the ice cream house. She also had the most delicious caramels which I made into lollipops by making them soft in my warm hands. I asked her if I could have a lolly stick to stick them on, and then I would climb up in my grandmother's birch trees and line up my lollipops.

I made a sign saying 'Lollipops for sale for 2 Danish kroner' and put it up underneath the trees. When my friends from the village walked by and bought them all, I had a big smile on my face as I put the money in my mother-of-pearl box with my seashells in it, and the box became a treasury of magical things always hidden in my grandmother's loft room.

The Flannel Nightgown

So many beautiful memories of my grandmother, even on her last breath of air. Uncle Helmer was sitting holding my grandmother's hand for her last hours of breathing life through her lungs. She was wearing a pink rose-printed flannel nightgown and my Aunt Gunver had been up to the florist in town buying flowers. When she took her last breath, my Aunt Gunver put the flowers in both her hands and told her brother Helmer and her sister Anne and my mother, that my grandmother had said goodnight forever.

My Aunt Gunver went into the kitchen after my grandmother's soul had flown away. She put the kettle on and made coffee for everyone.

They all sat in my grandmother's living room and talked about the old days and their childhood growing up in the house. My grandmother would have loved to have shared being there with her children around the table, but she was there in spirit. My mother and stepdad came to the house a little late after she had passed away, and sadly weren't able to say their last goodnight to her.

I will never forget the smells and the sounds in that house: the beautiful paintings my grandfather painted through his life, hanging on the walls; the swallows nesting in the outside toilet; the sound of the crackling fireplace; the sound of the old grandfather clock; my grandmother's footsteps across the floor; the family talking in the fine dining room; the patchwork cotton blanket she made for me which have travelled with me all over the world. But most of all, the hugs and kisses my grandmother gave me through my time with her.

I miss her . . .

CHAPTER 9

Shapes of Angels

Over time, moving out of Denmark in the late seventies and being away from my mother and living in England, I started to feel better about myself and settled into my life in England. But life started to change after me and Phil got married when he became more and more successful in the music world.

One cold winter day, sitting in front of my beautiful fireplace in my living room with the old Victorian ceramic tiles around it, I wrapped myself in my grandmother's patchwork blanket putting my bare feet close to the fireplace. I felt my gold ankle bracelet burning on my skin, but the soles of my feet felt warm after walking around in the cold winter garden in my lilac lace-up boots, and I began thinking and wondering if I should call my mother. I picked up the phone and dialed her number.

'It's me, Mum, how are you doing?' There was a long pause and straight away I felt uncomfortable calling her as I knew what was coming.

Her voice sounded sharp. 'Is everything okay?'

'No, nothing is okay, Mother. I feel very lost and lonely in my marriage and as you know, since Phil has become successful on the music scene, I never see him any more.'

Another long pause as I heard her deep sigh. 'You have a wonderful life and should be thankful for how your life turned out for you.'

I took a deep breath. 'But I miss and love you, Mum, and I have been wondering if you have found happiness in your life? I would love us to be closer to each other as it might also help me to find a way of resolving what is going on here with me and Phil.'

It got all silent at the other end and she hung up on me, and we never talked about it again until the day she became very sick with ovarian cancer. That was when she told me for the first time that she loved me. She was seventy-seven years old.

After the phone call, I laid myself down on the old couch, crying my eyes out; the only comfort was the beautiful burning fire where I saw shapes of angels in the flames telling me, 'You will be okay.' I fell into a deep sleep in front of the fireplace with tears still running down my cheeks.

When I woke up, I was feeling dry and very warm from the fire on my face and the loneliness was painful. I got up from the couch and put on the woollen headscarf my grandmother used to wear all the time in the strong winds when she walked me back to my house where she told my mother to be nice to me. I wrapped it around my neck for comfort and made myself a hot chamomile tea with honey to soothe my sadness.

CHAPTER 10

The Hairspray

I got a flight from London to Copenhagen, leaving my two boys behind to visit my mother in the hospital. She had been diagnosed with stage 4 ovarian cancer and I walked into the room which was filled with a beautiful scent of flowers. The window out to the garden was open and I could hear the birds singing, sitting in the willow tree. It took me back to having a tea party with my teddies under the willow tree. I would have liked my mother to have been there with me sharing the cakes I had made out of candy my grandmother gave me.

The wardrobe against the hospice wall was open a little so I could see all her beautiful designer dresses she hoped to wear again soon. All her makeup and of course her hairspray was on a little glass shelf above her big mirror. It took me back again to the moments of admiring her beauty and the smell of the hairspray falling over her hair so slowly, looking like little twinkling stars sparkling in her hair.

I put the flowers in a vase and put them on her little glass table next to her bed, which was filled with bottles of painkillers. 'I bought you single flower pale pink tulips as I know you love them so much, Mum.' She turned her face towards me, and I could see the reflection of her nearly bald head in the big mirror on the wall at the end of her bed. She looked very fragile and frightened in her eyes.

She said, 'Thank you for those beautiful flowers,' and she managed to sit up a little. I held her around her shoulders while she bent over to smell the sweet scent of the tulips. She felt so small in my arms as I laid her down in the bed which seemed to be too big for her now.

The nurse came in and gave her some medication to feel better, and she lightened up and wanted me to help her put on one of her designer dresses.

I helped her get the dress over her nearly bald head, and she suddenly looked at me and said, 'I'm so sorry for all the years we have missed seeing each other and not understanding how unhappy you were in your marriage. I'm worried for you going through a divorce right now, and what is going to happen to you and the boys.'

'It's okay, Mother, we are here now talking of love for one another and that is all that matters.'

She said, 'I would like to see Phil and talk to him.

'I promise I will try to call him and hope he will come and see you.'

She looked beautiful in her dress, and we put her little flat ballerina shoes on her feet. I gave her a little hand mirror so she could put on makeup and a little eye shadow on her eyelids. I put a pale pink rouge on her cheek bones, and we walked out to the garden.

We sat on a bench in front of a waterfall which had flowers around it, and the sound of the water felt so soothing to me as I wrapped us both into a cashmere throw I had given my mother on her seventy years birthday.

The Honey Story

My mother stroked my hair with her very fragile-looking hands, looking into my eyes saying, 'Do you remember when I spread honey on your sandwiches for you to take to school?'

'Yes, I do, Mother.'

'I'm sorry that I did that as I knew you didn't like honey.'

I stroked her nearly bald head and said, 'Mother, did you ever find out that I threw the honey sandwiches in the bushes just before I cycled home?'

'No, I didn't.' We both laughed and held each other even more tightly. She looked at me with tears in her eyes as she whispered in my ear with her very weak voice, 'I love you, Jette.'

I wiped the tears away and left them on my dress so I could smell her tears later and re-live the sensation of being close to her. That evening, after hugging my mother and kissing her on her forehead and saying, 'Goodnight, see you tomorrow,' she held my hand tight and I kissed her hand and walked out of the room. I went back to the hotel I was staying at and laid myself on the bed, crying with deep emotion.

I picked up the phone to call Phil who was on a tour in America with his mistress. He never answered the phone, and he never called my mother or went to see her before she died. I cried myself to sleep that night, feeling lonely and thinking of me and my mother at the hospital wrapped up together in the cashmere throw, feeling her heartbeat against mine and thinking, *Why did she never show me her love when I needed it the most?*

Was I relieved she would die? Was I sad? I knew in that moment that I wished for her to be in no more pain, and I felt some kind of relief myself, and hugged my pillow as I would have hugged my mother many times in my life if she had loved me for who I am and been proud of the beautiful little girl she had created. At that moment, hugging my pillow, I thought of my boys, missing them, wondering if they were doing okay without me kissing them goodnight.

She Squeezed My Hand

The next day came and I walked over to the hospital along 'The Lakes', as they call the four lakes in Copenhagen. I sat at a café having a coffee, watching the swans on the lake and joggers passing by, looking so fit. I felt cold and I wrapped myself in a blanket they had put out on the chairs. Anger came up inside of me, thinking *Why do all the people passing me look so happy when my mother is lying in a hospital bed, dying?*

It felt very strange listening to people talking around me, and the sound of voices laughing in the far distance felt painful to me - how could they not know that my mother was dying? I started to walk towards the hospital, and my body felt very heavy, walking in slow motion, feeling tearful, not knowing how my mother would feel and look today.

When I walked into her room, the nurses were changing the bed linen under her frail body, and she was making painful sounds as the cancer had spread through her body. She had bedsores in many places. I pushed a chair over to her bed and held her hand in mine and I told her that I loved her. She squeezed my hand tight and somehow I hoped that meant she was telling me that she loved me too. I was overwhelmed with emotions as it meant so much to me; at last, I felt a part of her love for me. I bent over to her face as she couldn't speak, and I kissed her on her cheeks and we sat there for a very long time, holding hands. I told her that I had to fly back to England that evening to take care of the boys, and if she wanted to pass over to the other side while I was here, she could peacefully do that while we were holding hands. She looked so peaceful at that moment in time with her arms crossed over her chest. I could see her heart beating underneath her dress as there wasn't much left of her body being eaten up by this awful disease.

I kissed her on her bald head and said my goodbyes.

The Christmas Card

It was late evening when I arrived home. I kissed both my boys goodnight and fell into a very light sleep. I got a phone call from my sister, Annette, the next morning and she told me my mother had died peacefully in her sleep that morning at 11am.

I laid myself down on my bed, holding tight in my hands a Christmas card she had written to me in December 2007. She passed in July 2008, seven months later.

Jette, you are such a beautiful girl who hasn't shone for a long time because of the relationship fading with Phil. But you should know that we all love you here in Denmark and you are worth a lot more than you think. You are clever and intelligent. You will find a lovely world without Phil and the sun will shine on you again. If I could choose, my children would always be happy. Kisses.

I read it over and over again and wondered why she could never say all these words out loud to me when she was alive? I keep the card close to me to this day as I know through her words that she did love me, and I feel comfort from time to time to read it out loud to myself. My love for my mother still confuses me as I have so many questions to ask her: did she find love in herself? Why did she find it difficult to love her children? So many unanswered questions. As I'm finding peace within myself about my love for my mother, I will hug her when I see her again among the stars, telling her that my life became full of magical moments, travelling the world seeing places I never dreamt was possible to see. My mother always talked about her dreams of travelling the world, but she never managed to fulfill her dreams before it was too late.

CHAPTER 11

The Old Sandals

We moved to Naerum, north of Copenhagen, when I was twelve years old. I felt very lonely without my grandmother nearby. I was put into a school ten minutes' walk from our house for the next six years. I didn't like any of my teachers as I felt I didn't learn anything. My German teacher, Mr Jeppesen, always smelled of old dust and wore clothes which looked like he had slept in them for days, always had the same old sandals on, and his toes were crossed over each other and had probably never seen daylight in years. I was fascinated by his way of walking on the tips of his toes, making this squeaky sound across the classroom every time he walked over to his desk. He always smelled of Aqua Velva aftershave which was so strong it made me sneeze out loud. He was not interested in teaching and always said, 'Why don't I play the guitar and you can sing along?'

Cotton Balls

I would fall into my dreams staring out of the window, while Mr Jeppesen would get his guitar out and start to play. I was looking at the concrete playground where the boys' and girls' toilets were located to the right of the dreadful, boring-looking iron gate which was locked through the day. That morning before the classes began me and my school friends were standing inside the girls' toilet smoking cigarettes. I was standing on a toilet seat so I could keep an eye over the toilet door, watching out for Miss Jensen walking around in the school yard. On that day she somehow walked in without me spotting her and one of the other girls whistled as a warning sign that she was near. I threw the cigarette in the toilet and pulled the toilet chain and rushed outside, and there she was in the doorway, looking straight at me with her angry brown eyes with a hint of hazel colour in them.

'Have you been smoking again?'

'No, I haven't, Miss Jensen,' I answered, looking straight into her eyes with my innocent angel face looking puzzled. Then I walked away with my school friends, feeling very grown up in my leather strap short kilt skirt and a very tight top which showed off the pointed black-and-white checked bra I was wearing. I would put little cotton balls inside the bra to fill it up as my breasts only fitted into a size 32A.

I was still looking out of the window dreaming while I could hear Mr Jeppesen playing a tune on his guitar in a distance, singing with his rusty voice a song I had never heard before. I came out of my dreams when I heard the school bell ringing and the lesson was over. I ran out of the door straight to the toilets, lighting up a cigarette, and thought to myself that the lesson speaking in German had been a waste of time.

Yellow Teeth

Chemistry was next after the break, and I hated my bald-headed teacher. He always wore black trousers that were too big with a belt done up to the last hole, and a T-shirt which had some kind of advertising sports name on it. He had awful yellow teeth and never smiled. He was violent to us pupils if we didn't pay attention to him. He once held one of the boys in the class up in the air by his hair, his feet not touching the floor. The boy was screaming in pain, and in slow motion I reached the classroom door and ran down the hall, looking behind me to see if he was there. I threw my home-knitted sweater on the hallway floor as the adrenalin ran fast through my veins. I reached the headmaster's door and just got through it before my teacher reached out to try and pull me back and away from the door. I told the headmaster what had happened, and the teacher was expelled on that day from the school. What a joyless school my parents had put me into.

Round Rings

I have many memories of the schoolteachers. My English teacher, Miss Larsen, had a nervous breakdown. She used to stagger across the floor on her very high-heeled red shoes, making these patterns of little round rings in the wooden floor. I was mesmerised by the art they made on the floorboards, and I would sit by my school desk trying to draw them on a piece of paper.

Miss Larsen would always say to us pupils as she staggered through the classroom, 'Sit down and be quiet!' She would sit herself down by her desk with her cup of strong coffee and put her hands around the coffee cup. I was entranced by her long, red polished fingernails. She would stand up and write with a piece of chalk on the blackboard, 'Page 3'. Her long nails were scratching against the board, and it made me feel funny all over my body. She always had bad breath from drinking too much alcohol.

She often staggered down the aisle between the school desks and stopped beside me, asking me why I was hanging over the desk. I would be dreaming and told her that I had just seen a big bird flying past the window, and I was wishing I could fly away with it. She wasn't amused and told me to stand outside the classroom door and say out loud the verbs from page 3. She would stagger back to her desk and cover her face with her hands and just sit there without a word spoken. I would sit myself down outside the classroom and my mind would be wandering off, sitting on a big bird's wings and the verb *I am, you are, he/she/it is* became a song as we flew away from the classroom up into the blue sky.

Russian Salad

The only teacher I liked in school was my Danish teacher, Mr Ibsen. He was a little eccentric and he had a long beard and a very friendly face. He would sit at his desk eating his lunch while he told us stories of Denmark's history, and I was always fascinated by the Russian salad in his sandwich which would fall into his beard as he was talking. He would sometimes do cartwheels between the rows of the school tables and his trousers would always fall down over his hips. His movements of pulling them back up made this scratchy sound like writing with charcoal on a noticeboard. He always praised my imaginative stories and told me 'You will become a writer one day. . .'

Save Our Ship!

Gymnastics was something I enjoyed very much. My gymnastic teacher, Miss Nielsen, was a big lady, who had this amazing way of walking through the gym room. Her trainer shoes were one size too big for her feet and she never did the laces up either. Her footsteps sounded like an army marching while her arms were swinging from side to side, brushing past her big breasts as her arms swung. I was fascinated by the swaying of her breasts like big waves rolling in to shore, and when I climbed up the ropes, I felt I was on a look-out deck on a ship and felt a little seasick. She said to me while I was at the top of the rope, 'Why are you not sliding down?' I called out, 'SOS!' (Save our ship!) and she scratched her head and said to me, 'Are you dreaming again?'

I slid down and was told to go to the changing room and take off my gym clothes and get dressed and wait for her to come in to see me. I undressed slowly for the boys to see my young body blossoming into a fully-grown flower. I knew the boys lay on top of the gym roof as there was a hole they could peek through to see us girls naked. As I put on my bra which was nicely folded with the cotton wool in each cup filling it out and looking like a bird's nest, the cotton wool fell out on the floor, and I heard the boys giggling. I gave them the finger and managed to put my clothes on quickly before Miss Nielsen came into the room to tell me to stop daydreaming.

CHAPTER 12

The Orange Fight

My best schoolfriend, Joan, lived just across the street from me. I used to walk to her house early in the morning before school began, picking her up and walking together to school. I always envied her having this lovely curly hair put up in little bunches, and lots of freckles covering her sweet little perfect nose.

One early Monday morning before school, I rang the bell at her house. The bell sounded like a bird singing and it made me feel good and I hoped that Joan would be in a good mood when she opened the door. Nobody came to the door, so I let myself in. Joan's mother passed me in the hallway: 'Hello, come on into the crazy house! I'm trying to get Joan ready for school!' As it happened, Joan passed me in the hallway really fast, chased by her mother. I put my arm out to stop the chase, and I was laughing so hard I could hardly stand up straight. The scene of those two chasing each other around the house was so comical, while Joan's mother shouted out to me, 'You go to school, Jette, or you will be late for class!'

I started to walk to school, which was only a ten-minute walk. I looked back over my shoulder, and I saw Joan running up the street with her braided hair swinging from side to side. Her petticoat was falling down over her knees and her school backpack was falling off her shoulder, scraping along the ground, and her shoes were falling apart. I had to laugh again when she called, 'Wait for me!'

'Why do you always get so uptight about walking to school, Joan?' I asked her.

'Because I hate school,' she said.

I put my arm around her shoulder and said, 'You're my best friend Joan,' and I hugged her tight.

'And you're my best friend,' she said. And off we went, our schoolbags hanging over our shoulders, covered with peace signs and flowers painted all over them.

We had some wild days of fun when her parents weren't at home. Once Joan got a sewing needle up into the heel of her foot after we had been chasing each other around the house. She was screaming in pain, and I said, 'Let me try and pull it out,' while we were both laughing and crying at the same time, seeing the funny side of what had happened. I managed to pull the needle out and the chase around the house began again. There were some oranges nicely arranged with other fruits in a ceramic bowl on the wooden dining table which was covered in a red and white chequered tablecloth, and we started throwing them at each other. The oranges somehow landed on the wall and the juice was dripping down towards the floor.

Joan said to me, 'We will be in trouble when my mother comes home.' Then she threw another orange towards me which somehow also landed on the wall. The wallpaper had begun to look a little abstract as we were bending over laughing our heads off, and as I was looking down at the floor, I saw Joan's mother's feet in a pair of white loafers standing right in front of me.

I stood up while Joan was still laughing. The heel on her foot had swelled up and her mother said, 'What have you done?'

I ran out of the door with orange juice running down my face and I tried to wipe it off on my school shirt before I had to face my mother in my house across the road. Me and Joan didn't see each other after school hours as a punishment for a couple of weeks. We hung out at school, though, in the toilets smoking cigarettes and being admired by the boys in the school yard. So many fun memories of me and Joan in our teenager years.

I met up with Joan a couple of years ago through my travels to Denmark, and it seemed a lifetime since we had seen each other after going our own ways in our late teens and we had both married and had our children. We recalled so many fun memories through our talk of the past when we were so young and free and running wild and didn't have any cares in the world.

The Tulips

When I turned sixteen, my first boyfriend, Vagn, who was crazy about the band The Kinks, gave me an album called *A Well Respected Man*. I had never heard of them, and we had invited a couple of friends over that night while my mother and stepdad were on their way back home from a holiday in Spain. I had a basement room in my parents' house, and we all sat on the floor around a dining table that we had cut the legs off and filled the room with big, bright-coloured velvet cushions. My record player was an old record changer which played multiple records in sequence without intervention, and for the first time I listened to The Kinks. I had a few old empty Chianti red wine bottles scattered around the room, covered with rainbow-coloured candles and the wax was dripping down over the sides. I had filled up the room with tulips I had picked from the garden, putting them in vases and was a little worried of what my mother was going to say. The tulips had a beautiful, sweet fragrance which made the room smell of springtime.

The Kinks

Vagn was wearing black, low-waisted bell-bottom pants, red suede zipper boots and a button-down flower-printed shirt. I was wearing green bell-bottom pants with a low waist and a very short white T-shirt, together with white mid-calf Go-Go boots with a block heel and a zipper. Most of our friends had left their shoes upstairs by the front door as my mother always told them to take them off, but I rebelled against taking my boots off as they went together with my outfit. The guys' feet always smelled as they didn't wash often, and the room would be filling up with the aroma of smelly socks and burning candles. The sweet scent of the tulips seemed to vanish in the air as we were surrounded by the cigarette smoke and the sound of The Kinks as the first record dropped down on the record changer was the song *All Day and All of the Night*.

It all stopped being fun as my mother suddenly stood in front of us, as I hadn't heard my parents coming home. She had bought a turquoise leather jacket in Spain for me, and she threw it in my face as I had forgotten I was supposed to make dinner ready for them both on their arrival home. She told everybody to go home and sent me to my room upstairs as a punishment, and that was the end of our little gathering listening to The Kinks for the first time. She strangely never mentioned the tulips.

Dating Jan

Me and Vagn broke up when I turned seventeen. I fell in love with Jan who lived in the same neighbourhood as me. He had the most beautiful red hair and always dressed smart in tailored brick-red twill pants and a bold-patterned zip-up mock turtleneck shirt, and he was known for always having a scarf around his neck. My favourite on him was an orange and gold-brown cravat tie scarf. He loved his brown pebbled-leather loafers and he walked like John Travolta in the movie *Saturday Night Fever*. All the girls in the neighbourhood wanted to go out with Jan. I remember the first time he showed the world that it was me he wanted to date as he took my hand and kissed me in front of our friends, and there were many disappointed girls in my town who had wanted to date him. I felt over the moon holding his hand in mine as we went to the movie to watch *The Parent Trap* with the actress Hayley Mills who played twin sisters. We held hands all the way through the movie and my hands felt very sweaty while we were trying to eat popcorn at the same time. How sweet and innocent those days were, and I had no idea at the time that five years later our time together would end when I packed my suitcase and said my goodbyes to him.

Jan's Swedish mother didn't like me and tried everything to split us up. Jan got very depressed as his mother was determined for him to study at Niels Brock business college in Copenhagen. He started to go there but it was too much for him and he started to take drugs and sat in his room all day listening to The Moody Blues. Little did I know that I would be living in the South of France twenty years later having Justin Hayward, the singer and guitarist of The Moody Blues, as my neighbour.

Our turmoiled relationship started to fall apart as Jan's heavy drinking and his behaviour became a big problem for me, and I found out that he had dated many other girls in those five years.

One night I was at his apartment, and I told him that I didn't want to be with him any more. The morning after was the day I bought the Sunday newspaper with the ad for an au pair job in London. I got the job and told Jan I was leaving for London the next day.

While I was packing my clothing, he was sitting crying his eyes out, begging me to stay and saying we should get married. I closed my suitcase and ran out of the door and down the stairs. When I got out in the street walking towards the train station, I told myself 'Don't look back' as he was hanging out of the window calling out my name.

I never saw Jan again.

*

My mother told me that she read in the newspaper ten years later that Jan had died of cancer, as his body had been eaten up by the alcohol abuse he had suffered from all these years. I did get a letter from his parents many years later saying that he never got over losing me.

CHAPTER 13

The Sanctuary of Living Things

Throughout my childhood living with my mother and stepdad, the house became a sanctuary of living things.

While I was doing my domestic chores as a punishment from my mother, I would open the kitchen windows and the breeze blowing the orange-coloured net curtains from side to side sounded like ocean waves coming into shore, and slowly moving out again. I would be walking in the warm sand, feeling the small grains in between my toes and laying myself down, looking up in the sky imagining faces in the clouds that smiled sweetly at me and blew me kisses, touching my cheeks before landing on the warm sand around me.

While I was doing my chores in the living room, I would sit myself down on our rusty-coloured velvet couch and look at the fish in the little aquarium which was standing on a black marble table built above a radiator. I always wondered if the fish felt hot in the water. It was just the right height for my deep hazel-coloured eyes to gaze into, which seemed to develop more brown around the iris as I grew into my teenage years. I became a little mermaid swimming among these elegant and vibrant-coloured fish of the sea, and I would forget all about doing my chores.

The bathroom would become my little paradise island. I would put the bath taps on and fill up the bath with soapy bubbles. I would lay myself in the bath and catch the bubbles in my hands and blow them into the air, visualising in the bubbles that I was lying in the fields feeling overwhelmed by the beautiful smells of freshly-cut grass, roses in bloom, birds flying in the sky, with the sound of ice cream vans and children losing their balloons into the clouds. I watched them getting smaller and smaller until they were little spots on the horizon disappearing into the unknown, and I always wondered where in the universe they were going.

While I was lying in the bath soothed by the warm, bubbly water, I pictured my mother standing by the bathroom mirror which had a frame of seashells around it. She would back-comb her hair with a rose-gold plated steel comb which I loved the smell of, as it smelled of my mother's hair spray, L'Oréal Elnett. It had a picture of a lady on the can with the same hairstyle as my mother's, and she looked like my mother too. She would spray it over her hair after she had put a shoulder cover on to protect her clothes. I loved that shoulder cover. It was pink and made of nylon and it had little fringes around the edges. I would sit and watch her putting it on and the room would be filled with the mist of hair spray, mostly landing on me and my clothing, and I would walk around feeling that I belonged to her glamorous world.

In the middle of daydreaming among the bubbles, I would suddenly hear my mother's sharp voice in the distance, and quickly get out of the bath and start to scrub it while all the colourful bubbles went down the plughole, ending my little journey of beach life and my mother's beauty.

My bed in my bedroom was my safety blanket where I would feel most comfortable under my duvet. It was covered in cotton linen which, in my imagination, had this overpowering scent of jasmine which lingered on my body. I would imagine myself in a beautiful long, white silk dress tied with a ribbon at the back, just showing a bit of my petite ankles with a delicate ankle bracelet I had made from a piece of white ribbon strung with the colourful seashells I kept in my grandmother's mother-of-pearl jewellery box.

I was dancing barefoot in a barn where my grandfather was playing the violin he had bought on a trip to Germany. The barn was full of people dressed in imaginative costumes made out of fine silk which made sounds like soft waves coming in to shore. The shells on my ankle bracelet would tinkle against each other while I was dancing between the people, feeling the heat of their bodies against my face, and smelling the scent of their perfume. . .

Dream Walking

When I was seven years old, I vividly remember walking to school from our house. It took half an hour to walk there and, being a bit of a dreamer, I often sat myself down under the big willow tree close to the school, imagining having my little friends for tea and serving colourful cupcakes on a plate with hand-painted roses on it. I would have three little wooden chairs and a table made of bamboo, with a tablecloth my grandmother had sewn from an old cotton dress of my mother's. It was pale blue and still smelled of the scent of my mother's skin.

We had a teapot I had made out of clay in school, glazed in a red colour, and it always dripped a little tea in the saucer when I poured it into the cups. I would dip a sugar cube in the tea as my grandfather did with his jasmine tea and give it to my scruffy little old teddy. He had very shiny brown glass eyes and one ear missing, and I slept with at night for comfort when I was feeling afraid of the darkness.

Coming out of my daydream, I would realise that I was late for school and had to run the last bit, feeling hot in my blue overalls with one strap hanging down over my shoulder. I always had to pull them up, even though it was easy to make them tighter so they stayed up, but I left them as I felt it was a cool look.

Two Ripe Melons

I made it to the old wooden gate which had beautiful green ivy hanging all over it, just before the teacher closed it. The teacher's name was Miss Olsen. She was a very tall woman, always wearing long flowery dresses and flat shoes. She took very long steps with each foot while her thighs were rubbing against each other, and her wide hips were swaying from side to side. I thought she was a beautiful woman and I wanted to look just like her. She had lovely wavy brown hair, always put up in a ponytail with a red silk ribbon in a bow hanging down over her shoulders. She had beautiful teeth and a lovely smile. Her breasts were fully shaped like two ripe melons pushing up under her dress, and the boys would sit daydreaming, hoping one day to meet a girl with such beautiful melons. She used to come out into the schoolyard, which was surrounded by birch trees and wildflowers in bloom, with a big bell in her hand, ringing like a church bell, telling us all it was time to go into the classroom.

Miss Olsen would always carry her black cat under one arm and a big clock under the other arm into the classroom. She would put the still snoozing cat on her desk, its tail with two white spots hanging down over the desk swaying from side to side, and it would make purring sounds which always soothed me into more dreams instead of listening to Miss Olsen.

I would hear her in the distance saying, 'Sit down, lovely children.' She was wearing these big round, brown-framed glasses which had a very strong lenses and made her eyes look twice as big. They always frightened me, and I would fall into my dreams, watching the big clock on her desk with the tick tock, tick tock sound, making me doze off quite nicely until she called my name out loud.

'Jette, are you listening?' I somehow managed not to fall off my chair and got my reading book out of my very scruffy black school bag which I had covered in a pencil drawing of a pair of Indian moccasins I had begged my mother to buy me on my eighth birthday. I loved them so much and often slept in them too. They were made of soft leather and covered in little rainbow-coloured pearls, hand-sewn into the leather, and tied with a suede ribbon. I was always told by Miss Olsen that I really must get a new school bag, but I loved the old bag as it was a part of me. The big clock on Miss Olsen's black wooden desk chimed every hour when the class was over, and we would all run outside to play in the garden which had so many hiding places when we played hide and seek.

I always hid underneath the jasmine bush with its over-whelming perfume which had a fresh feminine scent to it. I would sit there daydreaming time away, putting the flowers in my long, braided hair and was always told by Miss Olsen to take the flowers out before going into class again. I was quite argumentative and would ask her why, and sometimes she would shake her head and say, 'Okay leave them in, but stop daydreaming and listen to the lessons or I will have a word with your mother.'

Scratching His Balls

Going into the other classroom after lunch break, we had Mr Gunnersen who was teaching us History. He had awful bad breath and always scratched his balls on a corner of his desk while he was telling the class to open up our books.

I was fascinated by the movements he made, swaying from side to side and always wondered why he did that. He was a bald-headed, very skinny man, always dressed in bright colours: brown suede shoes and a very dark blue velvet jacket with a yellow polo-neck shirt, and cream trousers held up by a brown belt with a fancy buckle on it. When he sat down, I could see his fancy rainbow-striped socks which reminded me of a lollipop.

Petticoat

I wasn't interested in History and always fell into my dreams of walking home from school, which became an adventure in the wintertime when there was a lot of snow lying on the hills. I would forget the time as I was sliding down the hill in my woollen dress and thick tights and big black lace-up boots where I had taken out the brown laces and put bright red laces on them. I had a petticoat underneath my dress which my mother forced me to wear. I would slide down the snowy hill and my petticoat would get heavier and heavier with little snowballs inside the little holes of the design of the petticoat and, they would turn into ice. I would walk home at a very slow pace and knew my mother would be angry at me for forgetting the time.

Hot Chocolate

I would go to my grandmother's house first after the fun of sliding down the hills and I would sit in front of her fireplace, having taken all my clothes off which were soaking wet from all the snow I was covered in. I wrapped myself in the cotton patchwork bedspread my grandmother had sewn on her sewing machine and used to lay on top of my grandparents' bed.

She would make me a hot chocolate so my body could get warm, and I loved sitting on the old chair next to the Aga. The seat was covered in a red velvet fabric my grandmother had sewn on her little sewing machine and it felt so nice to sit on it as I knew it used to be one of her dresses from when she was young; it was a comfort to me, warming my little bottom on it. She would pour hot water onto the melted chocolate first and stir it before she put hot milk in it. She would give me a small spoon with melted chocolate on it and it was heavenly delicious. I would drink the hot, milky chocolate in front of the fireplace, listening to the old hand-carved oak grandfather clock standing in the corner next to the fireplace, with its pendulum making this wonderful slow sound, like a heartbeat, swinging from side to side. It made me feel very relaxed and ready to face my mother's outburst for being late home from school.

CHAPTER 14

The Factory

My years in school were full of dreams of being a dancer. I loved ballroom dancing and went to classes for a while and ballet too. I was never encouraged by my mother to keep dancing and I was told to go out and get a 'proper' job after I left school at eighteen. So I did.

My first job was in a factory sitting making little machinery parts for air navigational transmitters for pilots to use in the cockpit at the front of an aircraft. I would just do the job automatically without thinking and I would disappear into my own little world and imagine that I was dancing on stage in a rose-pink cotton dress falling softly against my body, floating across the room, expressing my body in contemporary dance. It made my job so much more interesting as the little knobs I had to put into the same holes a thousand times came to life and would start popping out and dancing on the belt in front of my eyes in their little white dresses and ballerina shoes and my dreary job became much more fun and time passed quickly.

My dancing daydreams became my lifeline, helping me cope with my job for a year. I used to travel to my job on my little scooter, leaving my parents' house early morning. My route to work led me through the forest with the most beautiful birch trees swaying from side to side, coming to life and dancing in front of me with their silver-coloured leaves looking like little pennies, making sounds like a trio of musicians playing on Vangoa banjos.

Impulse

One day, I woke up and got on my scooter, heading for work through the forest as usual, and I had a sudden impulse to turn left instead of right, and I headed for the coast. I loved the feel of the sea air as I rolled along, watching the seagulls flying by, and wondered what to do as I so badly wanted to leave my job as it was leading me to nowhere land.

I stopped at a little ice cream house and bought myself a cone with two scoops of vanilla and one scoop of chocolate, thinking, *Should I have whipped cream on top?* I was watching the little children making castles in the sand with their buckets and spades while their parents were sunbathing. The smell of sun cream overpowered the smell of the sweet ice cream as it touched the tip of my nose. It felt sticky but at the same time it cooled my windswept face where hundreds of freckles had reappeared after so much sunshine as I went along on my scooter. I decided to make the day an adventure.

As I was finishing my ice cream, licking the last bit of sweetness from around my lips, I looked around at the little shops across the street and spotted a sign in a shop window, saying they were looking for a full-time assistant.

I headed over and walked into the shop, finding a heavily-pregnant woman standing at the counter. She had the kindest face and a lovely smile, showing a row of perfect teeth which nearly blinded me with their whiteness.

She asked me my name and she told me her name was Anna. She explained that she was leaving the shop to have the baby a month later.

She asked me if I had worked in the fashion industry before. I said no I hadn't, but I could learn from her and assured her that it wouldn't take long for me to learn how to run the business.

She listened to what I had to say about leaving my job in the factory and I knew I was determined to never go back there ever again. She gave me her beautiful smile and said, 'Can you start next Monday?' I jumped up in the air with joy and felt like I was on a cloud nine - and a new chapter in my life began.

I said, 'Thank you so much!' and hugged her and asked if I could touch her gorgeous stomach which was as round as a football.

'Of course you can!' she said. I put my hands on her very warm body and I felt the baby kicking against my hands, perhaps welcoming me into his life. Anna told me it was a boy, and she would call him Charlie. Little did I know that many years later I would give birth to my son called Charlie.

My life turned around that day from being a factory girl to a fashion girl. I never went back to the factory again and my dreams of becoming a dancer grew stronger every passing day.

CHAPTER 15

The Morning Newspaper

On the day of my twenty-third birthday on a beautiful April spring day, I was sitting in a café, happily enjoying my little feast of coffee and an almond croissant. I was having a break from my work in the fashion world which I had begun to find very boring, just giving my all to being a saleswoman, trying my best to sell clothing and at the same time fulfilling people's need for interactions with me, telling me their life stories and somehow hanging on to life through me.

I was reading the newspaper and for some unknown reason I started reading it from the last page where people were advertising for nannies and au pairs. One caught my eye: an English/Danish family were looking for an au pair in London. I called the phone number, and this Danish lady answered the phone saying she was in Copenhagen visiting her mother with her three children and did I want to come for an interview later that day? I said yes that would be fine!

I went along to see the family and the interview went very well. The next thing I knew, I was on a flight to London leaving behind my boyfriend, my family and the job I had had for four years.

Arriving in London

When I arrived in London, I had no idea that I would never go back to Denmark to live again. A journey had begun of exploring the world of travelling, roads which would take me to places I would never have imagined.

Seeing the bridges across the Thames, Big Ben, the rainbow-coloured rooftops appearing through the cotton clouds that evaporated into thin air as we got closer to landing, was the most exhilarating and exciting beginning of the journey taking me to another world, walking on English soil.

*

I was welcomed by the family at the airport. Their three boys were running towards me with their arms up in the air, all wanting to hug me at the same time.

Driving through the streets of London, I was looking up into the sky trying to count the clouds passing by while the boys were talking to me in the north London accent I had to get used to, and I kept pinching myself that this wasn't a dream.

We arrived late afternoon at this beautiful three-floor Victorian house with a wide staircase leading to the front door. I counted the steps as I walked up towards the house and it came to seven steps. Those steps would give me many stories to tell of the family I was going to work for.

Rooftops

I unpacked my things in my very small room which was located on the top floor. The first thing I put up on one of the sloping walls was a drawing my little sister, Annette, had made of a ballerina when she was only seven years old. My room became my little sanctuary of dreaming of becoming a dancer.

I opened the little rooftop window in my room to find a whole new world out there with rooftops and front doors painted in all rainbow colours. What an amazing sight. . .

I wrapped my bluebell-coloured silk scarf around me which my mother had bought me many moons ago. It was falling softly around my shoulders and the smell of my mother's perfume on it somehow made me miss her while I was dancing with joy as the beginning of a magical mystery tour was unfolding itself.

Checkers Game

My first day of waking up in my little room I was listening to the sound of pigeons sitting on the rooftops cooing welcoming me to the house. I got into my blue faded jeans and a white cotton summer top with no sleeves and my old pink trainers which had no laces in them. I put my hair in a ponytail and slid all the way down from the third floor on the winding oak wood bannister, passing the gold wallpaper on the walls which became like a warm sun shining on my face every day as I landed in the softness of the dark velvet-textured chocolate-brown carpet.

I would start the day making breakfast for the three boys before they headed off for school. I would walk the youngest three-year-old to his nursery school, which was only five minutes down the road.

We would count all the different shaped trees with their long arms reaching out to us as we were passing them. We counted the trees every day, and he quickly learned to count to ten. He really liked me as we got to know each other. He would come up to my room and just slip into my bed in the mornings with his little one-eyed teddy bear with one of its legs hanging to one side after being dragged along the wooden floors through his first three years of being a little boy. I always remember his straight hair swaying from side to side as he ran across the wooden floors in the house, running towards me with his arms stretched out to the sides for me to grab him and lift him up in the air without any fear of falling.

I would start the day making beds on the second floor, opening the windows so I could hear the birds in the trees singing. It became a tune while I was making the beds, 'See the birds fly high in the sky, when you and I will try to come by.'

The living room had a beautiful original oak floor from the Victorian days, and massive windows from floor to ceiling with gorgeous pastel sage-green shutters. The tubular flowers of a Japanese honeysuckle peeking through the vast open windows would overwhelmingly fill the room with its sweet fragrance and the sun would shine through the windows making a design on the floor like a chess pattern game. I would forget about the chores, imagining I was wearing a dress with a black and white chess pattern design on it. I would turn into a ballerina, jumping into the boxes and pretending to be both players fighting against each other. My little pieces would jump out of my dress, flying into the air before landing in the dark boxes, and the battle would begin to unfold. Who of the two players would win?

I would get interrupted by the lady of the house asking me what I was doing dancing around and not getting the chores done! I came back into the real world and my dress would fall to the floor, as by magic my jeans and white top would cover my body and my trainers slid themselves back onto my bare feet.

Battenberg Cake

When I finished my chores late afternoon, the three boys would be arriving home from nursery and school. They were walking through the hallway, throwing their school bags up in the air, and kicking off their muddy shoes in the hallway on the dark chocolate-brown velvet carpet I had to hoover every day.

I would have to prepare afternoon tea for the boys who would be starving after a long day in school. I would make them peanut butter and jam sandwiches for their tea, and slices of the very English Battenberg sponge cake which had a pattern of chequered pink-and-yellow squares held together by apricot jam and covered in marzipan.

I would build a little house with the slices of cake and try to balance it on a plate as I walked into the dining room on my forever-favourite old trainers which were falling apart. I would put the cake onto the dining table next to the delicate, fragile Chinese teacups, hoping it wouldn't fall over. Me and the boys would sit down and imagine that there was a family living in the cake, and we would knock on the door, asking politely if we could please eat a piece of their delicious house until all the slices were eaten. Then we would imagine that the family would disappear into a little hurricane, lifting them up in the air like in the movie *The Wizard of Oz*, looking for another house to live in somewhere else in the vast universe.

I always had another imaginative story of the Battenberg cake each day when the boys arrived home from a mentally tiring day at school, wanting to disappear into a little bit of fantasy world with me.

*

Life in the house became fun for me, and the boys always had a new adventure on the horizon; they looked forward to what I had in mind for their next adventure in the house. The boys had a playroom full of toys and a rope hanging from the ceiling which helped them to forget their tasks in school. We would play Tarzan and Jane and swing from side to side on the rope and disappear into the jungle surrounded by cute monkeys and birds singing flying around us. We would drink coconut milk from the palm trees, holding hands and dancing around the bonfires we would make on the beach.

The Stripy Toothpaste

At bedtime, I would disappear into the moonlight with the boys and the delicious hot cocoa I had made for all of us. I would bring them up to my loft room with the glorious view over London's magnificent rooftops. I would open my windows and wrap the boys in my bed linen to keep them warm until they were told by their mother to go and brush their teeth which always turned into a battle of who could get the most toothpaste out of the tube before their mother came in and told them off.

The experience of setting their wonderful imagination free and being creative, writing their names in toothpaste on the beautiful antique Victorian carved mirror was one of my lessons into the unknown world of fun for the boys.

After the battle in the bathroom, the boys would be running up the wide staircase finishing their cocoa drinks, ready to watch the moonlight with their big smiles, showing their white teeth which were no longer white as the cocoa had made a very decorative design on their teeth and the boys were ready for sleeping until dawn dreaming of stripy toothpaste.

The One-Eyed Teddy

The youngest boy would crawl into my bed in his blue and white striped pajamas with his teddy, still missing one eye, dangling against the floor, hoping that he could sleep there with me for the night. I would carry him into his bed when his eyes were closing and his breathing was slowing down, knowing that he wouldn't wake up before dawn with his teddy close by his side. I had promised him that I would find a new brown eye to be sewn back on so teddy could watch the moon with us with both eyes every night.

*

After working in the house for about a month, I found out that the husband of the lady of the house was a well-known musician. I had been wondering who he was and why his wife never told me anything about him, only that he was a musician, and he was touring a lot with the band he was in.

One early morning getting ready to do my chores, I put on my gorgeous original Lakota beaded moccasins with soft leather laces I had bought at the colourful vintage market in Camden Town in north London. I put on my old scruffy Levi jeans which had big holes in them after being washed a thousand times and being worn night and day, and my beloved old cream-coloured Danish fisherman's sweater I had worn since I was seventeen, bought in a quirky little shop back in Copenhagen's little side streets of Nyhavn. The harbour was filled with fishermen's boats which always felt comforting to me as I would listen to the fishermen talking about the catch of the day and the aroma of the tobacco they were smoking in their pipes filled me with a feeling of bliss.

Dreaming of all these memories inspired by my clothes, I would open my little rooftop window watching, the vibrant orange colors of the morning sunlight, shining on the rooftops of London Town. I would watch the birds flying high while I brushed my teeth and braided my hair ready to do the chores in the house.

I would slide backwards down the bannister from the fourth floor to the kitchen and would make myself a piece of toast with lots of butter on it and a spread of homemade raspberry jam. I would lick my mouth for the sweet taste of a few crumbs left over on my lips, and drink a coffee from my favourite mug with 'Jette' written on it. It had white roses painted around the letters and was a present the boys gave me on my birthday back in April.

Meeting Dave Davies

I walked into the living room carrying the Hoover, and as I put it down on the beautiful oak wood floor, I looked out through the window to the street in front of the house. While I was hoovering the long, draped curtains, they always amazed me with their beautiful bright colours of moon-blue and violet-coloured roses and fluorescent green leaves, filling up the silk material that fell to the ground, swaying elegantly in the breeze that came through the vast windows which I always opened while I was doing my chores.

As I was looking out of the window, I saw a classic black Fairway taxi stop at the front of the house and a man got out, wearing blue bell-bottom jeans and a red velvet jacket with a red and blue floral-patterned shirt. He was wearing high-heeled olive-green suede boots with a zip at the back, and a dark blue cashmere scarf which draped softly over his shoulders. As he ran up the never-ending wide staircase, jumping every two steps, the warm breeze blew his very long hair from side to side covering his face and it was not until he walked into the hallway that I realised who he was. His hair fell softly over his shoulders, and he took off his dark sunglasses and I could see his face clearly. It was Dave Davies from The Kinks.

I had this instant flashback of my first album *Kinks*. The picture on the cover of four guys in frilly yellow shirts and fox hunting red jackets, wearing black suede high-heeled boots with the zip at the back.

And here he was, smiling at me in the hallway. . .

CHAPTER 16

Cup Of Tea, Love?

Dave's mother, Anne Davies, gave birth to her children in a house in north London called, by coincidence, Denmark Street, me being a Danish girl. . .

The song 'Sunday Afternoon' which her other son Ray had written with the lyrics 'I got a big fat mama' was ringing in my ears as I walked through her door. She was always sitting in a big old armchair, filling up the chair with her wide hips which had carried seven pregnancies and a few miscarriages through her life.

The fireplace was always burning with the kettle hanging above the fire and she would always say 'Cup of tea, love?' which fascinated me as she would pour the tea into a cup with plenty of milk and sugar, while we would sit and talk about her girls and the boys, Dave and Ray, who were born ten years after the girls.

We would always have Digestive biscuits to dip in the very strong tea and I would look at her deep, dark eyes which made me a little uncomfortable. She had not many teeth in her mouth, and she told stories of Ray and Dave, how they started out playing across the road in the pub, 'The Clissold Arms', when they were very young boys. She would tell me stories of how she would rise early in the mornings and iron their yellow frilly shirts for their gig nights around London town when they were very young.

Their father, Alfred Davies, I only met once at Dave and Lisbet's house. He was a very skinny man with a mouth that smiled from side to side, and he had a big, crooked nose. He was wearing big lace-up boots and denim overalls and he was also famous for sitting in various pubs in Muswell Hill drinking beers after work. There is a bench with their mother's name, Anne Davies, engraved on it, in Fortis Green Road in north London.

On a warm summer night in the late eighties I was in Ray's house with the family sitting in the living room talking of all the good times and fondest memories of their mother Anne who had died peacefully sitting in Ray's armchair by the window...

CHAPTER 17

The Clissold Arms

I had an interesting and liberating experience while I was living in Muswell Hill, when I met up with my lovely yoga teacher and dear friend, Ellen, at 'The Clissold Arms'. We went into the room where they had filled it with memorabilia of The Kinks. Family pictures covered the walls, and the faces of Dave and Ray were printed into the fabric of the black-and-white couch. We ordered a glass of sparkling wine and sat ourselves down on the couch celebrating my freedom after the divorce, and we had a giggle sitting on The Kinks' faces. . .

Healing on the Mat

We also celebrated the yoga class I did with Ellen, finding myself again, finding out who I was as me, Jette. She would put a roll of paper in the middle of the room and roll it out and she would ask the students to write a word that meant something in our lives right now. I wrote 'integrity' straight away, and somehow, I didn't even have to think about it. It was like something was lifting my soul into understanding what kind of relationship I had had for so many years with Phil.

'Integrity' stands for 'honesty' and implies a refusal to lie or deceive, trustworthiness, and incorruptibility to a degree that one is incapable of being false to trust.

I realised at that moment that I had not had any of those words for most of my marriage. My teacher Ellen asked me if I wanted to stand up and talk about what the word meant to me. I stood up feeling vulnerable and very emotional and tears were falling on my cheeks while the words came pouring out of my mouth about the years of betrayal, of my husband being unfaithful for years in our marriage. But more interestingly, I was talking of the self-worth of my own value as a human being, my self-esteem, my self-compassion, my self-acceptance, my self-respect, my self-confidence, my self-love, my self-care. . . I could have gone on and on.

It was all taken away from me through mental abuse, years of feeling ugly, fatigued and worthless. It was a revelation and somehow a disclosure of talking to the other students openly of my desire to change things around for me to be Jette again.

After the class was finished some of the women came up to me saying 'Thank you for being you,' and hugged me. One woman said to me that she was determined to go home and talk to her husband about their life together, about things that have to change and set some boundaries between them. I was overwhelmed by the effect that my talk about the one word 'integrity' had on all these beautiful women.

CHAPTER 18

Covered in Butterflies

I started to seek counselling from a very dear lady, Jasmine. I would get in my car and drive to her place after dropping my two boys off at school. While I was driving through the beautiful countryside, I felt very fatigued and uninterested in life's journey and had the sensation that I was covered in butterflies all over my body which had been sitting tight on me for a very long time.

I would sit on her very inviting olive-coloured couch where I kind of disappeared into the huge cushions and wrapped myself in a warm throw I had brought along. It felt like a safety net against the fear of finding out who I really was as me, Jette. Words would pour out of my mouth; I was asking Jasmine questions, not realising that I answered them all myself as she never said a word to me. The only two words she said to me were 'Stop saying sorry' and 'Phil'.

I would get up after an hour in my warm, safe little spot on the couch and say my goodbyes and I felt so much lighter driving home.

After several months of seeing Jasmine, talking freely of the dazed and bewildered life I had been leading for far too many years, I would open the window in my car as I drove home and let one butterfly fly off into the fields of wildflowers every time I had been to see her.

Slowly I felt I could breathe again and bit by bit through my time with Jasmine, I started to feel free of the past and a sense of a new beginning, of being me, Jette, started to unfold itself. I would hug my two boys so tightly when I got home; I hugged the walls and the things I loved in my house, and I felt the heavy, black clouds above me had lifted for good. I began to believe my journey in life would show me the way through doors closing and doors opening with adventures ahead of me of travelling the world and it all came true.

I realised after I divorced Phil that I felt so relieved and full of excitement for new beginnings in my life. My relationship with my boys became calm and peaceful, as there was no more drama in the house. I started to choose my friends carefully and lost all the negativity around me of so-called friends who turned their back on me after the divorce.

Sunny Afternoon

Three years after my divorce, I went to the theatre with my Danish school friend, Marianne, who was visiting me in my sacred nest in Muswell Hill to see the show 'Sunny Afternoon' by The Kinks. We sat in seats close to the stage. The show began and the dancers came on stage and the band started the show with the song 'Sunny Afternoon'.

It was strange for me to sit there watching the actresses who played the sisters of Ray and Dave. One of their sisters, Joyce, was so familiar to me as she had been my mother-in-law for thirty-four years. I fell into my dreams of seeing Joyce cooking the Sunday roast in her kitchen, always singing in her beautiful operatic voice, and she would always wear a shower cap on her head so her hair wouldn't smell of food, which always made me and the boys laugh.

Her Sunday roast was to die for. She always cooked in the same lard over and over again, and the roast potatoes were the best potatoes I ever had; her homemade apple pie with custard cream was mouthwatering to even think about. So many days and nights were spent in my mother- and father-in-law's house. Ken, her husband, would tell stories of when he was working as a policeman in north London. Joyce would make funny faces behind his back as she had heard the stories a million times before, and me and the boys laughed so much it hurt our stomachs. Those memories will always stay with me wrapped in ribbons in my heart.

They both passed away many years ago and my little grand-child Sophie's middle name is Joyce. I wish she could have seen her little grandchild today as Sophie will pass her name on through generations to come.

After the show was over, me and Marianne went for a drink in a pub close to theatre and we were talking of all the memories I have had being a part of the family.

CHAPTER 19

Pineapple Dance Studio

As the days went by in the household I was living in, taking care of the boys and doing my chores, I would in my free time take the underground train into the centre of London where I discovered all the beauty of dancing. I had heard of the place called 'Pineapple Dance Studios' which I had walked past a thousand times before I had the courage to walk through their doors and ask at the reception if they had classes for beginners?

I did join a class eventually, and I used to love walking around the streets in colourful Covent Garden which was full of cafés where dancers would hang out, drink coffee and listen to live music, and sometimes would get up and dance. When I started to hang out in these places, I would sit and watch the dancers dressed in black leotards, rainbow-coloured legwarmers and black tap shoes, get up off their chairs and begin to tap their feet to the music. I would imagine I was in the movie *Funny Face* with Audrey Hepburn, surrounded by sweaty people dancing in smoky rooms. The pianist would tap his feet to the rhythm of his long fingers that touched the keys and produced notes he softened or sustained with his feet on the pedals.

It was magical to watch, and I dreamed one day I would be one of the dancers floating across the room with ease, hardly touching the worn-out wooden Victorian floors where thousands of people had walked and danced over the years.

A Quirky Shop

Through my dancing classes and dreams of becoming a dancer, one afternoon I visited a quirky shop close to the house where I was working for the Davies family. It was a cold day and I had put an old woolly scarf around my neck that I had found deep down in the second drawer of my hand-painted blue, green and yellow striped chest of drawers, covered in little stickers of sunflowers which I had found in the quirky shop.

The lady who owned this interesting little shop was a very eccentric-looking woman. Her name was Eliza and she fascinated me with her odd, whimsical and quirky way of moving around, like a little scatterbrained green-haired fairy wearing ragged clothes, with a crocheted sugarloaf hat, and Tinkerbell slippers which made sweet musical sounds as she walked across the room. She had three striped, ginger cats who always sat on the desk. As I walked by, they would purr, hoping I would stroke them as they gazed at me with their large, deep eyes. I read once that when their pupils were narrow, it meant that they felt contented and wanted to be stroked continuously.

It was a shop I would go to often, to be inspired by the quirkiness of it. I felt comfortable telling her of my dancing dreams, and she would lend me a pair of light pink ballerina shoes, and a romantic tutu to wear. I would put them on, and I felt like a 'dancing queen, young and sweet, only seventeen'. I would pick up one of the cats who had one black eye; the other eye always seemed to be half closed, looking like a pirate in his stripy ginger fur. We would take to the dance floor, gliding down the old wooden floor, while the eccentric Eliza would get out her little antique violin and play along in time with my feet touching the floor. It was magical to dance in Eliza's quirky shop and I forgot all about time until I had to head back to pick up the youngest boy from nursery, still dreaming of becoming a dancer.

Dedicated Follower of Fashion

As time went by, after doing my chores at the house, picking up the boys from school, sharing my magical world with them, at nighttime I would be getting on the underground for my dance classes and hanging out with my friends at the local pubs in north London near where I lived, drinking pints of beer and smoking my bamboo pipe.

One night, Lisbet and Dave asked me if I wanted to come with them to watch a gig where her husband's nephew, Phil, was playing with a band at a theatre in London. I said yes, I would love to, and ran up the stairs, taking two steps at the time, ending my journey on the fourth floor in my rooftop room, wondering what to wear. I slipped on a wool mini skirt in the most vibrant yellow colour, and a green sleeveless top with a ribbon trim, a pair of brown suede knee-high boots, and a bit of sparkling jewellery around my neck.

I put my hair up in a ponytail, and grabbed my large, dark brown leather handbag, and to finish it off, I put on a pair of round dark blue metal-framed John Lennon glasses, all bought in Carnaby Street. I felt like the song 'Dedicated Follower of Fashion'. I went into the boys' rooms on the third floor and kissed all three of them goodnight. The youngest boy had dropped his one-eyed teddy on the floor, and I picked it up and promised him that we would find a matching eye at the downtown sewing shop when I was picking him up from nursery the next day. I put the teddy underneath his blanket close to him and kissed the teddy goodnight too. The son of the next-door neighbour, who was a priest in the local church, was babysitting that night. I walked the last two flights of stairs down to the ground floor hall with care as my suede boots had very high platform heels.

We drove off into the night in their white Citroen CX car with cream-coloured softly upholstered fabric seats which were very comfortable to fall into as I was dreaming of the excitement of watching Dave's nephew, Phil, playing electric guitar with the band.

We arrived a little late and sat down in the front row. People had to get up from their seats so we could get into the middle of the row. The spotlight hit us, and I looked up on stage and saw Phil looking at me with a big smile. Throughout the night I was hypnotised by his playing, and I felt my first extra heart-beat of attraction to him. I spoke to him briefly after they had finished playing and said my goodbyes.

I was in heaven all the way driving back home to the house, looking at the stars in the sky which seemed to be brighter than ever, and the full moon was shining down at my smiley face. I could see the reflection of the little patterns it made across my face in the car window.

That night was the beginning of my and Phil's attraction for each other. I remember running up the staircase as we arrived back at the house, feeling as light as a feather. While I was undressing, I felt on top of the world. I put on my old blue and white stripy pajamas on, which were made of a soft cotton fabric that felt like silk on my skin which my dad had given me for my sixteenth birthday. As I opened the rooftop window in my room, I felt a cool breeze touching my face and neck and I wrapped myself in the cotton blanket which still had the scent of my mother's perfume. I sat on the edge of the window, looking out over the rooftops, dreaming of what a magical night this had been.

Through the year I worked for the Davies family, I started to see Phil most days, and he would come round when I was babysitting at night, and we would sit holding hands on the old couch and it became a sweet romance between us in our early twenties. . . looking back we were so very young.

I would go with him when he was playing gigs in clubs and theatres. I was also introduced to his music friends and that's how I met my dear friend, Annie, from Liverpool; we're still close friends to this day after forty-five years of friendship.

Saying my Goodbyes

As time went by, working for the family and having many adventures with the boys, I knew I would have to say goodbye very soon as I would be leaving after a year of being their au pair. I had been their companion through fantasy, imagination, fun, sadness and tears at times and happiness through laughter and a lot of hugging. I hope I gave them a little taste of what they could achieve, and that anything they desire and dream of is possible.

Dance Classes

As I left the Davies family, Phil and I decided that I should move into his parents' house. We were inseparable as we felt madly in love with each other. We had very little money and were adjusting to life with his parents. We had a small bedroom in the house filled with his electric guitars, old school blazers with old exam papers still in his pockets, and teacups under his bed. I started to imagine them coming to life and finding their own way to the kitchen; I would point my magic wand at them before they found their way into the old worn-out wooden cabinets which had been opened and closed a thousand times.

I started to feel a little locked into a world of pleasing Phil, as the doors seemed to close behind me one after the other, but no doors opened ahead of me as I became less creative as the years went by. Somehow I hung onto my dance classes for some years and I did join a little theatre group in London which gave me a little push back to my passion for dancing and acting. We did a show called 'Going Hollywood' where I played Shirley Temple and we did a lot of dancing numbers from that era, along with singing. It kept me in the moment of being me, and the years went by, mostly doing dance classes in Covent Garden, and some performances from time to time around the London area.

Living in my boyfriend's parents' house was a challenge as there was not much privacy in that little bedroom we lived in. I would wake up and kiss Phil good morning, stumbling over his guitars, and find my way down to the kitchen where I put the coffee on and headed for the shower which took hours to heat up. I would run back to the bedroom as the house was always freezing cold in the mornings and try to find my dancing clothes as the sunrise tried to shine through the windows, all misted up from the moisture in the air that had developed through the night. I would jump back into bed to feel warm for a minute or two, feeling the body heat of Phil who was still fast asleep. Finally, I would slip on my sweatpants and my rainbow-coloured leg warmers, and fill up my bag with my flat lace-up jazz shoes, towels, a packet of cigarettes and a shiny-looking blue flask filled with water. I would run to the underground station, which only took ten minutes, but I always missed the train I was supposed to be on.

My leather bag with the long, worn-out strap, carried a heavy load of dancing gear every day through rainy days and sunny days, which had faded the leather. Five minutes late every day, I would throw the bag into a corner of the room before putting on my jazz shoes. They had slid across the worn-out wooden floor where so many other feet had touched it over the years that it had started to smell of the blood, sweat and tears of us dancers, as we expressed our heart and soul through our dancing.

The Phone Call

One early morning before I opened my eyes, sleeping with one leg over Phil's body as I always needed space to breathe through the night, knowing in my dreams that I would be on the hard wooden dance floor the next morning warming up for the dance routines, I heard Phil's mother's voice. I thought it was another dream as I heard her calling out for her son, 'There's a phone call for you, Philip!' She always called him by his full name.

I whispered into his little curled-up ear, which he had been sleeping on for hours, 'Wake up, you have a phone call.' He managed to get his jeans on, still with his eyes half closed, and ran down the stairs wondering who it could be. I curled up feeling cold without the body heat from him and pulled the duvet over my head.

Seconds later I dreamed he was whispering to me, 'Wake up! Wake up! I just spoke to David Bowie's manager who wrote "Wild is the Wind"!' I thought I was dreaming but I wasn't, and we both curled up together talking of what had just happened! He had asked Phil if he could come and play on Iggy Pop's album *The Idiot*, which David Bowie was co-producing. It was the beginning of success for Phil as a guitarist joining the Rock and Roll world.

David Essex

Phil's first real tour was in 1976 with the pretty heartthrob of a guy, David Essex, who had a big hit with 'Hold Me Close'. I went to see the band play in Copenhagen, and I remember sitting in the front row, and listening to the screaming girls throwing themselves over the balconies to reach out for the singer, and breaking bones in their falls. On our way out of the theatre, I was in the same limousine as the singer, and a crowd of girls thought I was his wife. They grabbed me by my hair trying to pull my hair out as a souvenir, and the long dark blue velvet dress I was wearing with my brown suede knee-high boots was ripped as they try to pull it off me. Somehow, I got into the limousine feeling all shaken up thinking that I have had a taste of fame and paparazzi following you around. . .

CHAPTER 20

Bohemian Furniture

We moved out of Phil's parents' house and into our first apartment in north London in the late seventies. We filled it up with our taste of bohemian furniture: a big couch covered in green cotton fabric with a design of wildflowers on it. We had lined curtains made for the bedroom in a dark red velvet colour as we were famous for sleeping until noon, and the curtains kept the daylight out. We filled up the windowsills with feathers, candles, glass bottles in all shapes and colours, and wildflowers in vases. The bookshelves were filled with albums of the old blues sounds of Muddy Waters, BB King, The Beatles, The Rolling Stones, Eric Clapton, Dire Straits and of course, Phil's uncles, The Kinks.

And how amazing that many years later in the early eighties, Phil would play with many of these bands through the years to come.

CHAPTER 21

Blue Moon Tea Rose

Phil introduced me to my dear friends, Annie and Paul, back in 1975 when I still lived in the house where I was an au pair. We met in the house of an old friend, Alistair, where at the time, Annie's boyfriend Paul lived. Many years later Paul would join The Moody Blues as their keyboard player for over twenty-five years.

I always remember the entrance to Alistair's house as he had the most beautiful blue moon tea rose in front of his gate which smelled divine as you walked up to his house. Alistair was a very eccentric guy, always wearing tight 1960s spike pants a little too short, and you could see his very white legs in a pair of black lace-up work boots, and his too-small T-shirt, which had seen better days, looking very tight around his stomach. He always smelled of cigarettes and showed his yellow teeth and he had lots of long curly hair.

Alistair had a small studio at his very funky house for bands to rehearse in, and you could hear people rehearsing in that room, from the kitchen area. Later I realised it was Annie Lennox and Dave Stewart with their first band The Tourists, way before they became The Eurythmics. We didn't know then that Phil would play with Annie Lennox many years later. I remember when I was introduced for the first time to my dear friend Annie in Alistair's kitchen in 1975. She was wearing brown velvet loon pants with red stars on them, and a pale pink angora jumper she had knitted herself. I found out she had been knitting her own jumpers since she was very young and made most of her own clothing herself to make them original. That day she was wearing suede pastel platform shoes. I could tell that she came from Liverpool, and she had a very deep blood-red lipstick on, and always put more lipstick on before she got into a car. I always asked her why she was putting on more lipstick, and her answer was always, 'just in case,' which became a fun joke between us. I couldn't understand the Liverpudlian accent she spoke, even though I found it very charming. Friends thought I was from Liverpool as we spent so much time together over the next forty-five years, getting married within a year of each other, and both of us having two children over time.

I remember when Annie was pregnant with her first child, Amy. We were sitting in her living room talking, and as it happened, I was telling her a joke and she laughed so much that her waters broke! She told me to get her a pair of clean knickers while she sat there on the toilet and I couldn't stop laughing. Off she went to the hospital and Amy was born that night.

When she was pregnant with her second child, Hannah, I was pregnant at the same time with my first child, Oliver. I remember when she came to my house one day, as we now lived in the same neighbourhood in north London, I was six months pregnant, and she had just found out she was pregnant with Hannah. She stared at me with a bewildered look in her eyes and told me, 'I need a cigarette and something strong to drink,' and we both laughed out loud.

One day we were sitting in her living room having a cup of tea, talking about fun times before we had children, and we suddenly realised that baby Hannah (her second child) was sitting in her bouncer in the kitchen, and we had forgotten all about her! We rushed into the kitchen and she was bouncing up and down quite happily with Peter, her little teddy I had bought her when she was newborn. We got Hannah out of the bouncer and gave her many cuddles and we giggled so much that Annie nearly wet her knickers which was another fun joke we had many times over through our long friendship to this day.

Hannah is now in her thirties and has kept Peter to this day, and he wears a knitted jumper with his name knitted into it. He has been lost a couple of times in various places in the world but has always been found again and sent back to Hannah.

These moments in time are so precious to me when I think back on them today. The stories of Annie growing up in Liverpool until she moved to London in 1975 were so exciting to me, as Annie was born in Forthlin Road in the Allerton area of Liverpool. Paul McCartney of The Beatles lived at one end of Forthlin Road, and Terry Sylvester of The Hollies lived 500 yards from Annie's house in the other direction while they were growing up. Annie told me that she would put her autograph book through Paul McCartney's letter box hoping for a signature, but sadly his dad would return the autograph book unsigned.

John Lennon lived two miles away from Paul, on Menlove Avenue, and that house is now owned by the National Trust and open for tourism to this day. When they were renovating John's house, Annie's brother gave some of the original fixtures and fittings from his house to the National Trust. He lives in a road which backs onto John Lennon's house and also borders the wall of Strawberry Fields that John Lennon wrote about.

John Lennon wrote the song 'Strawberry Fields Forever' in 1967 with a double A-side single, 'Penny Lane'.

Amazing to think that years later, I would pay a visit with my mother-in-law, Joyce, to her brother Ray Davies' apartment in New York in the same building were John Lennon lived. I would also meet Paul McCartney and many other celebrities walking up the wide staircase at Buckingham Palace.

CHAPTER 22

The White Hart Pub

Me and my dancing teacher, Kathy, decided to take a trip to New York to experience classes with Alvin Ailey, a choreographer at the Alvin Ailey American Dance Theatre. It was my first time in New York and flying over the town late at night was magical, with all the tall buildings rising up in the sky as if they were coming out of the sea. The overwhelming beauty of the 305 feet tall Statue of Liberty made of copper on the outside, in all its glory on Liberty Island in New York Harbour, shone its beauty from underneath the clouds while we were circling over the city watching all the twinkling lights, and I felt so excited to experience New York!

My friend Anne Grethe I had known from when we were both au pairs back in London was now living in Upstate NY. She picked us up from the airport and we stayed with her in her house in a town called Katonah. While we were driving to her house, I fell into my dreams of the time when we were au pairs together. We would meet up in 'The White Hart' pub in the town of Southgate where we both lived. We would be wearing scruffy faded jeans and big jumpers and Danish clogs on our feet, and we looked very Danish. We smoked a pipe as it was cheaper than cigarettes. I loved the smell of the tobacco we blew out into the room, making it a little hazy for the boys to see us clearly. They were always waiting for the Danish girls to arrive and buy us pints of beer - not half pints, which shocked the boys. I loved the atmosphere in the pub where people interacted with each other, talking about life's experiences.

I thought of the times when Phil would pick me up from college in the town where I lived. I was studying English language as au pairs were supposed to do. He would be wearing his old jeans and a very old, cotton T-shirt that was far too small for him and an old blue army coat which was falling apart. The Kickers shoes he was wearing with a bit of a heel, impressed me as I had never seen such colourful shoes before. The first time my mother saw him at Copenhagen station, arriving from the UK, she said to me, 'It must be him in the blue army coat. He looks like a musician.'

Air Balloon

Coming out of my dreams, we arrived at my friend's house in Katonah. It was nice to meet her husband, Tom, an American guy who was in the children's clothing business, and they already had two beautiful children. Over the next few days, we would travel on a train into the centre of New York to do Alvin's classes. Me and Kathy would go to Greenwich Village, which was a bohemian hang-out in those days. It blew my mind that all these amazing vintage shops and restaurants had the best food in town. We would walk through the city watching the police on horseback riding through town, trying to keep order with the traffic and handbag snatchers and sadly, beggars, constant anti-violence demonstrations and other political issues, people hoping for peace (as we do to this day) which sadly, always seemed to end up in violence.

Looking up in between the skyscrapers to see the blue sky above and being in New York overwhelmed me with emotions of joy and how lucky I was to experience the beauty of this city. Me and Kathy climbed the narrow staircase inside the Statue of Liberty's torch made out of copper which is covered in a thin layer of 24 karat gold leaf. The fear of heights gave me bruises up my arms as I walked up the narrow steps, clinging on to the handrail. It was worth the bruises as the view over New York City was spectacular, and you felt you were in an air balloon way above the clouds, looking down on all the twinkling lights of New York. It was a moment in time of the excitement feeling on top of the world, I would treasure in my heart forever.

Alvin Ailey's dance classes were an experience of self-awareness of your body structure and the balance of your mind and soul, floating beautifully across the room with an elegance that made it look easy to the eye. I loved his classes and learned to appreciate how important it is to be aware of how the natural rhythm of your body works.

I returned home to England after ten days in New York where Phil and I decided that we wanted to get married in Denmark. We both returned to the US three years later as a married couple when Phil was asked to record at Caribou Ranch in Colorado.

CHAPTER 23

Dusted in White Snow

We woke up one morning three days before the wedding and got into the car, a yellow two-seater Jensen Healy sports car, and drove to Denmark, crossing the sea by ferry from Dover to Esbjerg. When we arrived in Esbjerg, the snow on the ground was pure white and twinkled like little stars. I felt I was in a dream of sitting next to Father Christmas on his sleigh drawn by reindeers heading for the starry sky, stopping at the red brick chimneys on every rooftop in the villages dusted in white snow. The children would be in their warm beds, covered in patch-work quilts, not able to sleep for the excitement of opening up their Christmas presents wrapped in colourful Christmas paper with glittery ribbons. The presents would fall down the chimney and land under the Christmas tree and the children would be dreaming of their wishes of new toys, shining bright under the Christmas tree in the moonlight.

Ankle Bracelet

Falling out of my dreams of being on a sledge with Father Christmas, I suddenly felt cold and wet around my legs, as the snow on the roads had leaked through the floor of the car throughout the journey. Me and Phil were pleased to arrive in Copenhagen late at night feeling tired and very wet around our jeans, and our desert boots were ruined. We were staying at my mother's house, and we fell into a very deep sleep and woke up at noon the next day with the most beautiful warm sunshine smiling at us through the windows, and the snow had melted, and we both were very excited about the wedding preparations for the actual wedding the day after.

My mother and I went to the florist to get my wedding bouquet of wild daisies. As I stood there looking at myself in the mirror, trying on a string of daisies made to hang randomly down my long hair, I started to daydream of being a little child again.

I was sitting in the newly cut green grass with its overwhelmingly divine scent of summertime, making a little ankle bracelet out of yellow buttercups growing wild in the grass. I would make one bracelet for each ankle. I had a silk scarf my grandmother had made for me from an old dress she used to wear when she was a young girl. I can still hear her sewing on her old sewing machine, tapping her foot up and down with her old leather slippers covering her feet, worn out from carrying her babies on her hips, all seven of them. Her worn-out crooked fingers from years of being a farm girl were controlling the stitching of the emerald-green dress which was being made into a beautiful scarf for me. I would put it up to my face against the warm sun shining on me, feeling the magic and wonders of faeries and angels filling up the sky. I would dance around in the grass on bare feet, and the feeling of the wild yellow buttercup ankle bracelets against my skin felt soothing on this hot summer day. I would lay in the grass and feel the warmth from dancing as my pale rose coloured silk dress clung to my body.

I would get up and run to the stream and put my feet in the water to cool down. My little ankle bracelets would fall off and the wild buttercups would float down the stream and I wondered how far down the stream they would end up.

My mother was shouting at me in the distance saying, 'Are you listening?' I turned away from the mirror and realised the wild daisies had fallen out of my hair, landing on the floor in a little circle and I put my feet inside the circle feeling I belonged to them. My mother pulled me away from the flowers and we said our quick goodbyes to the florist lady and headed back to my mother's house.

Love Letters

The morning of the wedding day arrived, and it was my birthday too. I looked up at the bedroom door and there was my wedding dress, a bohemian Laura Ashley white silk dress with tiny little daisy flowers sewn into the fabric, hanging there in all its glory waiting for me to put it on.

Phil was sleeping soundly next to me, and I whispered in his ear, 'It's our big day!' We stayed in bed talking about how we had met through his Uncle Dave. I started to daydream about being back in the house where I had worked for his uncle's family.

I remember the first time Phil walked through the front door. He was wearing scruffy old blue jeans. He had a big red comb in his back pocket for his very long hair which hung down to his waist, and to me he looked like Jesus. One very warm, sunny day, he invited me to come with him for a drive in his Jensen Healey car to Wimbledon to watch the tennis tournament. We had the roof down on the car, and we were holding hands while we drove through London town. The warm breeze was soothing to my face and my hand was getting sweaty and I was trying to let go of his hand.

I remember we wrote little love letters to each other every day after that first day of holding hands. I still have them wrapped together with a red silk ribbon with a big bow and a dried daisy from my wedding bouquet. I keep them together in a little wooden box my dad made for me when I was a little girl. I painted the box green with little yellow flowers on it.

I remember the times in his Uncle Dave's house when I would get out of bed wearing my favorite striped soft-woven cotton pajamas my grandmother gave me. I would sit myself by the open window in my little room, opening it a little wider, and climb out onto the rooftop and sit myself down reading my love letters for the pigeons which were happily cooing away. . .

I suddenly heard Phil calling me in the distance and I came out of my dreams, realising that I wasn't dressed and we were late getting ready for the church where all my family and Phil's family, who had arrived the day before from England were, sitting waiting for our entrance into the church.

My father was waiting for me outside the church door. I kissed my husband-to-be, and he went in ahead of me. I could see him walking up to the altar and the Danish priest welcoming him into the church.

I put my arm through my dad's, and we walked up the aisle and my dad looked so proud of his beautiful daughter getting married. He let go of my arm and kissed me on my cheeks and I now stood next to Phil who had a big smile on his face, looking straight into my eyes. The priest asked us to kneel down while he was looking at my plunging neckline. He conducted the wedding in Danish and Phil was a little bewildered, wondering what he was saying to us. Both our families were sitting in front of us on either side of the altar looking at us, which made us both feel a little uncomfortable.

Caribbean Island

I started to fall into my dreams imagining being on a Caribbean island while trying to concentrate on what the priest was saying to us.

I dreamed we were on a Caribbean island, standing underneath the swaying palm trees, just me and him making our vows to each other, putting rings made out of coconut shell on each other's fingers and listening to the waves coming into shore. I would be in an ebony-coloured silk dress clinging to my body, holding a little bunch of wildflowers in my hands, my long hair blowing around my face in the warm breeze. He would be there with his full beard and long hair, wearing his old scruffy jeans and a vibrant blue silk shirt, both of us barefoot and feeling the warm water and the sand between our toes.

Wedding Night

The priest was still looking down my plunging neckline as he asked, 'Will you take this man to be your wedded husband?'

I was married now, and we walked out of the church as husband and wife. The rest of the day was a blur to me as everybody in the family got drunk at the dinner reception and I just wanted to hide in a corner. But we did the first dance on the floor and cut the cake. When everybody had gone home to their houses or hotels, me and Phil were sleeping on a foldout couch in my parents' living room. Through our wedding night, people went to the toilet every five minutes, passing through the living room where we were sleeping. Not the most romantic wedding night to remember. . .

CHAPTER 24

My Car Ashley

We had no money to go on a honeymoon and life began as a married couple full of expectations of what life would give us, and exploring the world together. I kept my dancing classes alive and drove into London most days in my shades-of-brown coloured Morris Minor 1000 which we bought from a family who needed money for their very sick child, and I told them that I would take good care of the car. I called it Ashley from the movie *Gone with the Wind*. I loved watching the movie in my childhood and I would slip into my dreams as a child, pretending to be Scarlet O'Hara falling into Ashley's arms: 'Ohh Ashley, I love you, I've never loved anyone else.' It followed me through life as well as the line, 'After all, tomorrow is another day.'

CHAPTER 25

The Mushrooms

I was driving home on a very warm full moon night, after sweating through dance classes at Pineapple Studios in London. I came to a red traffic light but didn't stop as I was fascinated by the mushrooms growing in the back of my Morris. I crossed the road junction and was stopped by a policeman on the other side of the road. He asked me if I realised that I had just crossed the road on a red light. I got out of the car wearing my black leotard and striped cotton leg warmers. I had taken my dance shoes off, driving barefoot. He looked at me with a confused expression and I said to him, 'Well, can you see the mushrooms growing around the windows at the back of my car? I was looking in the rear-view mirror and I was wondering what it was, and I crossed the red lights at that same moment. I was wondering if they are edible.' He took his hat off and scratched the back of his head with his very big hand where I noticed on his ring finger a beautiful white gold ring with little stars on it. He started to laugh, showing his very crooked teeth, and said, 'I thought I'd heard it all, but this story is something else. I will let you off but please, put your dancing shoes back on and take a slow drive home.'

He had a big smile on his face and then he told me to remove those mushrooms as they were not edible! I put my dancing shoes on and asked him if he wanted to dance. We danced around a lamppost, and I said my 'Thank you for letting me off' and waved to him through the jungle of mushrooms looking at me through the rear-view mirror.

This is a true story; life in the late seventies was a much more peaceful and humane time to be young. I can still see his face filled with kindness as he walked away very light-footed, and I hope I made his day walking the streets of London worthwhile.

CHAPTER 26

Large Breasts

Phil and I moved to a townhouse in north London in the late seventies. He became more successful in his music as time went by and I kept the dancing up. He got a phone call one day from a producer asking if he was okay with going to Caribou Ranch in Colorado to record with an American singer. Before we knew it, we were on our way to the USA.

We arrived at Denver Airport and were picked up by a very young Teresa who worked at the ranch. She was wearing a green Hawaiian shirt and a pair of white shorts and lace-up trainers, and had beautiful long, curly hair. We got into the automatic gear-shift truck, and I was amazed by the way Teresa was sitting with one leg up under her other leg and one foot down on the accelerator, steering with one hand.

I was tired and my clothing was sticking to my body after a ten-hour flight from London. I was wearing pink dungarees and a white T-shirt and turquoise suede lace-up boots. The band's bass player, Andy, and his wife, Pauline, were sitting next to me on the back seat of the truck in silence, blown away by the beauty of the mountains. I had no idea this was going to be my hometown many years later.

We arrived at the ranch and put our stuff into our bedroom. There was a seven-foot-tall stuffed bear standing outside the bedroom in a corner. I felt very sad as I hate anything to do with stuffed animals. In the middle of the room there was a very large, beautiful cedar wood log bed with a beautiful Dakota patchwork quilt cover on the bed and there were sounds of native American music through a little radio which made the room very peaceful.

It was a magical time of exploring the mind-blowing nature of Colorado. One day my friend, Pauline, (the bass player's wife) and I were riding on horses in the mountains overlooking the beauty of the pine trees, and the deep valleys around us were breathtaking. Pauline was wearing a very short white top and faded blue jeans, and was riding in front of me and the horse suddenly decided to gallop. Pauline didn't have a bra on, and she had rather large breasts bouncing from side to side over her shoulders, and she was not able to control the horse. I was laughing out loud trying to hold on for dear life on my own horse, which started galloping too.

I saw pine branches coming fast towards me and tried to bend down or lean from side to side, hoping to make it back to the ranch in one piece. The beautiful stallions knew the way back to the ranch, galloping all the way, and we had no control over the horses at all and hung on for dear life, me still laughing my head off. We tried to get off the horses in an elegant way back at the ranch but kind of slid down to one side, and walked like the actor, John Wayne, swaying from side to side with a big gap between our legs as they were very sore on the inside of our thighs and were hurting for days after. That was our first experience of horse riding and it took days for both of us to get our legs close together again.

Blue Note

Teresa also sang and did catering at the ranch. We decided one night to get up on stage at The Blue Note nightclub in Boulder, doing backing vocals with the band We went to Teresa's house to practise singing for the gig, and we put Rickie Lee Jones on the record player. We had so much fun, not knowing that this was the beginning of a forty-five-year long friendship.

We drove little motorbikes up to the mountains and swam in the lakes while all the other wives of the band stayed back at the ranch sunbathing on the deck, waiting for their husbands to finish recording. I never really understood why they did that; I had a great time exploring a corner of Colorado. The amazing thing was that forty years later, I would meet James who became my husband. He also played at The Blue Note in the eighties when he was in a band called The Rave, and Teresa had seen him play there in those days before I met her. The synchronicity of me and him crossing each other's paths through time is something that can never be explained. . .

CHAPTER 27

Hormones Running Wild

After living in our house for four years, our first son Oliver was born at Portland Hospital in London.

Phil's Uncle Dave's wife, Lisbet, was taking me to the hospital in their old white Citroen CX which was a four-door fastback saloon car.

I rolled into the passenger seat, trying to make myself comfortable, and reached out for an old cushion lying on the back seat to put behind my back. There was lavender inside of it and the smell somehow made me relax into the long drive through London; the traffic was a nightmare and Lisbet was trying to calm me down by talking to me about nothing, and her voice sounded very sharp and loud as my sense of hearing was twice as sensitive with the hormones running wild in my body through my pregnancy.

I felt the contractions becoming more and more painful and I asked Lisbet if she could not talk to me as I was trying to do a little meditation, focusing on my tummy and watching the movements of my baby through the sleeveless embroidered white V-neck tiered dress I was wearing. His tiny feet were kicking right up under my breastbone and I felt my breasts filling up with milk ready to give my baby his first feast of milk. I tried to comfort him by stroking my tummy with both hands and telling him we were not far from the hospital, and he would see the bright light of the world very soon.

My hair was wet with sweat as it was a very warm September day, and I tried to reach into my big leather bag which was lying on the floor in front of my car seat filled up with clothes and cosmetics and a few tiny newborn baby diapers with a cute design on them called feather breeze. I picked out from my bag a vintage linen handkerchief with hand-sewn yellow roses on it which my mother gave me when I was very young. I was thinking about my mother when I wiped the back of my neck with it, and the sweat was running down my front too, and made my white dress stick to my body. In the middle of the contractions, I was thinking that one day my mother would love me for who I am.

We arrived at the hospital, and I tried to put my brown suede thong sandals back on my feet as I had taken them off because my ankles were swollen. I couldn't get them on, so I threw the sandals out onto the ground where we parked and somehow managed to slide into them when I got out of the car. The nurse came out with a wheelchair and helped me to sit into it, and we entered through the big sliding doors into the hospital and rolled into a private room. They put me on a machine to monitor my baby's heartbeat, and Lisbet was asked to leave as she was still talking to me. As she left the hospital, Phil walked through the door.

Dreaming Through Labour Pains

I was in labour for fourteen hours, and I remember the Laura Ashley wallpaper design of beautiful trees in my room; it made me feel calm. I fell into my dreams trying to distract myself from the pain I was feeling.

I was in a forest among the trees picking lavender flowers and I would lay myself down in the grass feeling overwhelmed of the fragrant of the lavender. The sun on my face felt warm, and I tried to breathe deeply through my labour pains, in and out, while I was still lying in the grass, feeling the soothing breeze on my bare feet and feeling the cool grass in between my toes. I could hear the midwife in the distance saying: 'We need to get the baby out as his heartbeat is becoming irregular.'

Two years before, I had lost my baby boy in my womb; I had been four months pregnant, and I was afraid of losing my baby again. I saw angels flying above me trying to calm me down, wrapping me into their wings, protecting me. I felt safe under their wings, and I saw the little boy I had never held in my arms telling me: 'I'm here with you in spirit, Mother, and I love you and I will see you again among the stars.' I felt calmness coming over me while the midwife gave me an epidural and I gave birth to my baby boy within the next hour. What a journey. . . one minute I had been in a forest in my dreams, talking to my lost child among the angels, and the next thing I knew, I had a seven-pound bundle of a beautiful baby boy, Oliver, in my arms. His dad was overwhelmed with joy seeing this little miracle being born. I put him to my breast, and he happily drank the milk coming out so fast like a flowing stream. I felt relieved that he took to the milk so quickly while I was massaging his tiny, old-looking, wrinkly feet which had perfect tiny toes that wiggled up and down, feeling very contented against his mother's body. It was such an emotional moment in time; tears were running down my face and little teardrops fell on his tiny pretty head, and I wiped them off with the handkerchief my mother gave me. The smell of his pure baby skin clung to the handkerchief for days afterwards and I kept it close to me when it was time for me and my baby to bond even more closely through our first night of sleeping together, and somehow, I felt that my mother was with us through the night, and I still wondered why she didn't love me.

We had told the midwife that if I had a boy, his name would be Oliver, or if it was a girl, her name would be Sophie. As it was a boy, they put a little tiny blue name tag on his very small wrist saying, 'Baby Oliver'. I still have the little blue tag which fits on my two fingers if I put them together. I would never have guessed that thirty-five years later, Oliver and his wife Charlotte would have their first child born in 2019. . . it was a girl and they named her Sophie. . .

CHAPTER 28

Crystal Ball

The late seventies came around and my husband met up with Kenny Young, a songwriter who co-wrote the song 'Under the Boardwalk' which was covered by The Drifters in 1964! I had no idea that I would be friends with his wife, Judy, for many years to come and we are still close friends to this day. They lived near Oxford, and we went to their house often for long weekends. Phil was recording with Kenny and other band members, and they called themselves Yellow Dog and they had a hit with 'One More Night'.

I had many odd experiences of things that can't be explained in their house. We sat one night in the living room in front of the fireplace, and I started to get a headache. The guy next to me was a friend of Judy and Kenny and I felt he was somehow drawing thoughts out of my head, and I felt fear of what he was trying to do to me, so I walked outside.

He left the house later that night and I went upstairs to the guest room. It had a sink to the right of the room next to the beautiful cast iron bed and I turned the taps on to wash my face, and the sound of the water running through the plughole sounded like a river passing by. I can still hear that sound in my head to this day. I got into bed and covered myself with the patchwork quilt and dozed off into my dreams.

I woke up suddenly and sat up in bed and saw him standing at the end of the bed in the darkness of the room. He talked to me in a very deep voice, and I could picture his face in the dark. He had perfectly full lips and a very long, wide nose, deep brown eyes and long black hair. He started to talk to me, saying that I would be travelling later in my life to places I had been dreaming of as a child. And he knew I was unhappy in my marriage and to be careful of staying in a very unhealthy relationship.

I pulled the chain which had a little crystal ball in all rainbow colours at the end of it for the light to come on. He was not at the end of the bed any more. I never saw him again, only in my dreams one more time, many moons later, travelling the roads.

I was told by Judy that he died a few years later. . .

CHAPTER 29

Lazy Moon

Life started to change as I was meeting famous people through the parties Kenny and Judy had in their house. On a full moon night, they had a dress-up party I still have memories of.

I was wearing a blood-red colour velvet dress with a low-cut neckline, so my very young perky breasts were lifted, and I had my cleavage on show. The dress reached down to my ankles showing my fake tattoo (at the time) of a marigold flower on my left ankle. I had bare feet, and my hair was hanging softly over my shoulders. I was sitting by the stone fireplace in their living room, hypnotised by the sound of the crackling wood burning nicely, enjoying my glass of deep red wine with a floral aroma, with a few ice cubes in it.

I was putting the glass up to my very painted, plump, red lips when I had a tap on my shoulder. Turning around, it was one of the band members in Van Morrison's band asking me out for a date. I said politely 'No thank you,' as he did know I was married to Phil.

Van was a terrible driver, and I once drove with him to a local pub near where Judy and Kenny lived. He drove all the way to the pub in second gear, and when we sat down to eat food, I was sitting next to him at the table, but he never spoke a word. I looked away from him, and the next moment, I turned back and he had got out of his chair and disappeared *Into The Mystic*, the song he recorded in 1969 which was featured on his album *Moondance*.

So many fun moments at Kenny and Judy's house. One day, me and Judy were sitting admiring the photo-board of friends who had visited their house many times over the years, bringing back memories of the parties and fun times in their house. All us girls were looking very young, wearing clothing from the Biba shop in Carnaby Street in London, maxi dresses in striped patterns and lacquered leather boots, plaited long hair and large-brimmed, floppy velvet hats, and oversized sunglasses. The guys were in bell-bottom jeans, Jesus sandals, tie-dye men's tops, embroidered scarves and headbands.

As we were sitting there daydreaming of the past, looking at the old photos on the wall, a black guy who was doing backing vocals in Kenny's studio came into the kitchen and asked us in a very dark, dreamy voice, 'Where are the two of you from?' We answered that I was from Denmark and Judy from England. He had a big smile on his face and said, 'Well, standing in this kitchen we are delicious people made from black pudding, English muffins and Danish pastry.' We laughed so hard, and we held each other's hands and danced around the old kitchen table singing, 'Under the boardwalk, down by the sea.'

Barbados 1980

Memories of driving on the roads in Barbados in December 1980, where we spent a holiday together with Kenny and Judy, and two other dear friends Van Morrison's bass player, Rod, and his wife, Florence.

We had been driving along on the crazy, windy backroads in an old car with the old radio on full volume, singing along to a Beatles song. We were all enjoying looking through the dirty windows of the car, watching the turquoise Caribbean Sea coming into shore, with its twinkling stars reflected the light into my big round John Lennon glasses as we sang along. Suddenly we heard through this crackly old radio: 'We are interrupting this programme as we have just heard that John Lennon has been shot and has died.' We all went silent and could not believe what we had just heard. We didn't speak to each other for the rest of the day and we all just sat in silence on the beach looking out on the Caribbean Ocean which was surprisingly very calm. Eight years later I would be back siting on the same Gibbs beach, watching my baby Oliver running across the warm sand. . .

I have spent so many beautiful hours over many years in Judy and Pete's house in Wales where she lives to this day. Sadly, Kenny Young, who lived in the old house in Oxford most of his life, died last year in 2020. I would never have imagined that the first time I went to Kenny's house in 1978, I would spend some time with my now husband, James, forty years later in Kenny's second home, a beautiful earth ship in New Mexico. Life can be so full of surprises and that was one of them.

CHAPTER 30

The Manor House

My first encounter with Richard Branson was at a party at Kenny's house in Oxford. He was chasing me up the stairs in his groupie outfit (as the theme was roadies and groupies). He was wearing little red knickers and a blond wig. It was a wild party, but I managed to escape downstairs, and hide in the crowd.

I went to 'The Manor House' near Oxford for the first time in 1977; it was the first residential recording studio in England and owned by Richard Branson. It was fun sitting around with all the wives of the band members in the living room with the great big Irish Wolfhounds lying in front of the most beautiful stone fireplace. I was gazing out of the vast windows, looking at the lake Richard had put into the grounds. It was full of black swans sliding elegantly across the lake, and sometimes they spread their large wings and I would fall into my dreams of seeing *Swan Lake* at the theatre in London, the ballet composed by Tchaikovsky in 1875. The story tells of Odette, a princess who turned into a swan. I would sit by the window for hours, just watching the swans dancing on the lake.

The rooms at The Manor House were stunning. Each of them had a beautiful, vast fireplace, and the girls who worked at the house would make a fire in the rooms and I would sit in front of the one in my room with Oliver, my oldest son who was a little boy at the time. We would put a blanket on the floor and have a little picnic and I would read his favourite book to him, and he would be dozing off with his Pink Panther toy in his arms, and I would stroke his hair and doze off myself.

On our awakening, I would take his hand and walk through the long corridors into the vast dining room, where the vast oak table for fifteen people filled up the room and the old Victorian chandeliers hung over the table, and I could just imagine the Three Musketeers swinging from one chandelier to another across the never-ending table.

Chris De Burgh, who wrote the song 'Lady in Red' which became a big hit, walked through the room, as he was the artist recording at the studio on that particular day. Chris's wife, Diane, was pregnant at the same time as me with Oliver, and I remember walking through their house in Ireland, highly pregnant, and was amazed at the long corridors with lights which would turn themselves on or off as you passed them, one by one. Me and Diane became kind of friends until the day I saw her again at the Royal Albert Hall, backstage after Eric Clapton's Christmas concerts when Phil was in the band. I said 'Hi' to her, but she ignored me and walked away, to talk to all the celebrities in the room. That was the beginning of me feeling lost within my role as Phil's wife. I hated the world we had now started to live in, as I felt belittled for being who I am.

*

Coming back to Richard Branson, it was incredible to watch him becoming a British business tycoon and investor over the years. He married Joan, who was a brief friend of mine. I remember we used to sit in the kitchen at The Manor House back in the eighties, talking and giggling while having a glass of wine, with the fire roaring in the vast, stone fireplace the Irish Wolfhounds lying in front of it, feeling the warmth from the fire. It was an amazing and fun time hanging out at The Manor House with people before they became big names in the industries.

CHAPTER 31

Eric Clapton In Antigua

In 1988 we decided to take a holiday in December, travelling to Antigua with Oliver who was now four years old. I clearly remember the view over Antigua after a ten-hour flight. The turquoise Caribbean Sea was breathtaking and looked so inviting and I couldn't wait to swim in it.

The house we rented was set right on the beach on the south coast of Antigua. I settled into the house and picked some beautiful Caribbean lilies and put them in a vase by the open window. The white linen curtains around the windows were dancing in the warm breeze coming in through the open doors . . .

The first morning came, and as I opened my eyes, listening to the soothing sound of the gentle ocean waves, I looked at my son lying next to me, feeling the warmth of his little body against mine. His almond-shaped eyes were closed, and his long eyelashes fell so peacefully against his cheeks. His Pink Panther had fallen down on the turquoise-coloured tiled floor in the night. I picked Pink Panther up from the floor and put him next to Oliver and covered him up in the very thin white linen throw which had lilac-coloured edges, and I slowly slipped out of bed and walked out onto the warm sand in bare feet, wrapping my kimono around my body and dipping my toes in the warm, silky, turquoise water.

I sat down in the sand, feeling the warm sun on my face and I looked over my shoulder, seeing a man's silhouette in the distance walking towards me. He stopped and looked out across the sea and began to walk into the water in slow motion. His sunglasses reflected the warm Caribbean water and he walked out up to his waist and stopped and looked around. As he turned his face towards me, I recognised him, and it was Eric Clapton. He looked very peaceful, and I fell into my dreams of when I had seen him at a concert with a crowd of thousands of people listening to his magical guitar which gave me goosebumps down my spine. I remember he had this movement in his left foot, twisting his leg from side to side while his face showed all his emotions as he was playing 'Wonderful Tonight'.

Days went by and I saw Eric walking from his house up in the hills along the waterfront every morning, and I told Phil to have the courage to walk over to him and say 'Hi'. One day, I was sunbathing topless on a very soft beach towel, my hands playing with the warm sand falling through my fingers, when I looked up through my very oversized round, blue sunglasses. My floppy bohemian woven straw hat fell off my head as I saw Eric bending over me saying, 'Nice to meet you.'

I tried to cover myself in the towel and got up to shake his hand. He smiled at me and walked over to my husband who, without telling me, had had the courage to say 'Hello' to Eric who remembered him from when he played with Van Morrison back in Ireland many moons before.

We had dinner with Eric that night at the beach restaurant. It was a beautiful night and the small waves created by the soft winds on the Caribbean Ocean were so soothing to listen to. We had a beautiful night talking about music, and seeing Eric away from the limelight enjoying being himself was a moment in time I will look back at with good memories. Eric flew back to England the next day and a tour with him and his band happened for Phil not long after the unexpected encounter with him on a sandy beach in Antigua.

Life changed for Phil, becoming a successful guitarist after the world tour he did with Eric the year after in 1989. I also experienced a magical time travelling around with the band touring the world, and going to the White House in Washington DC was one of them.

CHAPTER 32

The Royal Albert Hall

The nights at The Royal Albert Hall in London, where Eric and the band were playing at Christmas time, were magic. I was being picked up in a limousine at our house every night and always had the same chauffeur. It felt lonely sitting so far away from him in this massive space of a car. I moved closer to where he was sitting and opened the tinted window.

'Do you live around here?' I asked him.

'No, I don't, I live in south of London.'

I looked at him closer and he was a big guy with a beautiful smile from ear to ear. He had a long ponytail and freckles scattered all over the top of his nose. He went on to say he worked as a builder in the daytime, and he had four children and a lovely wife who would be there tonight to watch the concert. 'How lovely,' I said, 'I hope she will enjoy the concert and maybe I will see her in the crowd.'

'Are you involved with the band?' he said.

'No, I am the guitarist's wife.'

He looked at me with his big smile full of white teeth reflecting in the streetlights we were passing on the roads; they nearly blinded me, they were that white.

'How long have you lived here in England?' he asked.

'Well. . . I bought a Sunday newspaper in 1975, back in Denmark where I am from, and they advertised for an au pair in London. I got the job and I travelled to England. I met my husband through the family, and we married two years later.'

He smiled at me in the rear-view mirror and said, 'What an amazing story of how you met your husband!'

'What is your name?' I asked him.

'I'm Michael. What's yours?' he said.

'My name is Jette, and it's been so lovely to talk with you, Michael.'

*

We arrived at the stunningly beautiful and distinctive Royal Albert Hall (named by Queen Victoria) which was built in 1867 in memory of her husband Prince Albert. Michael dropped me off at the backstage door where the security guys were standing. I said my goodbyes to Michael: 'See you tomorrow night.' I stepped out of the limousine touching the ground with my old brown suede cowboy boots which felt like walking in my old morning slippers, they were that old, and I loved them so much. I bought them on my first trip to Los Angeles in the early eighties, and I never found another pair the same ever again.

My long romantic, cream, cotton-flowered maxi dress fitted me like a glove. I had my long hair loose over my shoulders and wore a bohemian hippie felt hat with a golden pheasant feather my dad gave me many moons ago around the brim.

Eric's bodyguard Alfie came out to pick me up at the door. I always sat in one of the balconies close to the stage. I would walk around in the hallways looking at all these artists who had played here through time, and there were photos hanging there of The Kinks, and Phil was in the picture with Eric Clapton. It kind of felt a little lonely sitting in that balcony on my own, so I walked out to one of the bars getting a drink and started conversations with people. Mick Jagger was standing at the bar and Alfie, the bodyguard, introduced me to him as the guitarist's wife in the band. I didn't know what to say to him, and all I could think of was, 'Oh, you are not very tall!' He wasn't amused and I walked away and went back to my balcony and sat down on my seat waiting for the concert to begin.

Alfie was a real character; he was called the man with nine lives. He was a tall guy with a rugged-looking face and a big head of thick, curly, black hair. He had been in so many situations of being close to death, but he was a lovely kind man who took good care of me in many places around the world. I have fun memories of me and Alfie being on a flight to the USA to join Eric's band. We sat next to each other and as one of the stewardesses passed our seats to ask if we wanted something to drink, he started to tell her a story of him being a lawyer, and he was taking care of a legal case for me and Phil in court. He told her a guy in LosAngeles was being sued for harassment after pretending to be Phil; his wife coincidentally had my name, a story which I had told Alfie about, and which was, in fact, the truth. But he wasn't a lawyer but it did make me laugh out loud how he turned the story around to him being involved. He was a funny man and so full of stories to tell. . .

CHAPTER 33

The Helicopter Crash

On 27th of August, 1990 I had a phone call from Phil, calling me from the US as he was touring with Eric Clapton saying he was alive and don't read the headlines on the front of the English morning newspaper. I did read it and it said the American musician, Stevie Ray Vaughan, and three crew members of Eric Clapton's band were killed in a helicopter crash. Stevie Ray Vaughan did a guest appearance with his brother, Jimmy, at the concert. Alfie (Eric's bodyguard) was supposed to be going on that helicopter but was told he was too big and heavy and one of the other crew members took his place. It saved Alfie's life. . . it seemed that Alfie had been saved many times before in strange circumstances.

I went into my son's bedroom and told him that his dad was okay and hugged him. He wanted to come into my bed, and we just lay in bed hugging each other. My body felt cold from the shock of the phone call with the heartbreaking news, thinking that it could easily have been Phil on that helicopter. I put my cashmere throw around my shoulders which felt comforting, and I looked at my son's little round face, calmly falling into his dream world with his Pink Panther wrapped in his arms. I couldn't go back to sleep and watched the sunrise through my bedroom window, shining so brightly, making this shadow of a guardian angel on the wall. I lay down again next to my son and somehow fell into a dream of the guardian angel who has protected me and my family in many threatening circumstances that cannot be explained. . .

CHAPTER 34

Conor's Funeral

I remember one night at The Royal Albert Hall in London after the concert was over, I went backstage where Eric was standing with Conor in his arms and the paparazzi were taking photographs of them, one flashing light after the other. Conor's eyes were blinking constantly with fear of all the attention, and just wanted to be with his dad, hugging him tight. I thought it was heartbreaking to see Conor in the middle of the paparazzi taking one photo after another of him and his dad. And you could tell he didn't want to be there. . .

Many moons later, sadly we went to Conor's funeral. He was only four years old when he died. The funeral was held close to Eric's house. We went to Eric's house after the funeral and it felt very calm and peaceful. I was sitting on a couch in the living room listening to people at a distance and it became like a soothing mumbling in my ears. I was looking out of the window admiring Eric's beautiful garden, and I was thinking about life on the road. Entertaining big crowds of people, and not being able to spend much time with your family is the price you have to pay for being such a talented guitar player, as I found out myself, being married to a very talented guitarist.

I walked out on Eric's garden terrace and there was a beautiful white 'La perla' climbing rose covering the whole garden fence. It had a mild fragrance and as I was standing there smelling the rose, I looked across the terrace where Pattie Boyd, Eric, and George Harrison - Pattie's two husbands from the past - talking with each other. I felt quite overwhelmed to see these three people together, and I fell into my dreams of being a teenager listening to The Beatles and loving the song *Something* George Harrison had written for Pattie Boyd, and Eric's song *Wonderful Tonight* that he had written for her.

Night Club in Paris

I can look back on so many moments in time, fun moments too, on Eric's world tour. One night the band members and I were travelling in a limousine to a nightclub in Paris. We arrived at the door to the club and went straight to the bar. I asked the drummer, Steve Ferrone, who became a close friend through the years and is still a close friend today, if he wanted to dance. He wasn't very keen but said okay. While we were on the dance floor, I got a tap on my shoulder, and I turned around and it was the ballet dancer Mikhail Baryshnikov. He asked me to dance with him and I did! I was wearing a floral print spaghetti strap mini dress and a pair of white Converse All Star lace-up boots, and he put his arms around my waist and off we floated across the floor. He lifted me up above him, holding me under my arms, my long hair falling into his face. His big, strong arms lifted me even higher, and the music stopped and he gracefully put me down onto the floor and said thank you for the dance. I will never forget that moment in time.

CHAPTER 35

Back to Colorado

I was in my little cottage back in the UK on a warm spring day in 2016. I remember as if it were yesterday, walking into my little garden, laying myself in my hammock. I had a glass of smoothie in my hand, made of strawberries, bananas and a little pinch of almonds blended with a Greek yogurt and ice. The smell of my blue moon tea rose was overwhelmingly sweet and I took my sandals off and let my toes play with the dropped petals on the ground which felt cool on my feet.

My phone rang and it was my dear friend, Teresa, calling me from Colorado, asking me if I could travel over for her daughter Gwynedd's wedding.

I felt something inside of me that said I should go. What a lovely thought to visit Colorado too! I said yes to Teresa, I would love to come to the wedding. A month later, I travelled to Colorado, and I stayed with a friend of Teresa's in a small native American town called Niwot.

I landed in Denver on a beautiful warm spring day and Teresa picked me up. I hadn't seen her in over twenty-five years, but we had always kept in contact through letters over that long period of time, and she was the first friend I called after my divorce. We hugged forever and it was so good to see her face to face after so many years. We got into her truck and talked all the way to Niwot of the good times we had had back at Caribou Ranch all those years ago.

Chief Niwot

We arrived in Niwot, which is named after the Arapaho Chief Niwot who was a tribe leader during the nineteenth century. The name Niwot means left-handed.

I fell in love with this cute little town which has a population of four thousand people and a little Main Street with a few shops and a couple of restaurants and a bar. Over the next four years, though I didn't know it then, I would make many friends in a restaurant which seemed to be the hang-out for meeting up for drinks and talking for hours about life's journeys we all had taken. I also met James (my husband-to-be) at the bar three years later.

The bar was a place that reminded me of the TV series *Twin Peaks* as everybody knew each other and would talk about what had been happening in the town. At times we would have a fire out on the deck, sitting around and singing songs and maybe dancing too. The town reminded me of the western movie *The Good, the Bad and the Ugly*, as I imagine a few cowboys walking down the street in their Outback Trading Rawhide cowboy hats and rugged shaft leather cowboy boots, their Jingle Bob spurs ringing as they touched the ground along the path that followed the old wooden railway tracks.

I stayed at Teresa's friend's house in Niwot, and my youngest son, Charlie, was travelling over for the wedding. I showed Charlie around the town, and we would walk over to the area where they held concerts every summer, that they called 'Rock and Rails'. During those summers hanging out with friends at the 'Rock and Rails' every Thursday night, I would put on a floral western cowgirl dress with long, draped bell sleeves and a black Redhead felt riding hat and a pair of Laredo Bridget western boots. I would meet up with my friends in the fields, listening to great bands playing, and we would dance the night away while we watched the most stunning and mind-blowing sunsets over the mountains. I have put memories of those magical nights into my little magic box which I open from time to time.

Smoke Rings

I have lovely memories of the beautiful evening of my friend Teresa's daughter Gwynedd and Sean's wedding. My son Charlie and I would dance the night away. Teresa's husband T (short for Robert) looked so handsome in his suit with a butterfly tie, and he was smoking a cigar and was blowing smoke rings. I put my finger through one and I will always remember him saying to me, 'I hope that one day you will meet a man who will love you for who you are.' Neither of us knew that three years later, I would marry their neighbour, and would live in the same street as them.

Kathy's House

A couple of days later after the celebration of the wedding was over, I put Charlie on a bus going to Denver Airport as he was travelling back to England. I gave him a big hug and said I would be going back to England soon! But I didn't know at that moment of saying my goodbyes to Charlie that I would be living in Niwot on and off over the next three years. When I woke up the next morning ,I walked down to the end of 3rd Avenue. It was a cul-de-sac, and as I turned around to walk back to the house I was staying in, I looked to the right and admired this beautiful English garden in front of the house. The lady of the house came over to me and we started to talk, and I told her how I loved this little hippie town of Niwot. She told me her name was Kathy and she had an apartment in her house for rent, and I walked with her into the house and liked it straight away. I told her my name was Jette, and I moved in the next day.

CHAPTER 36

Little Bird

Niwot was a town where my life changed overnight. My next-door neighbours, Liz and Bruce, became very close friends. They lived in a beautiful, button-blue coloured painted house, with a western porch at the front of the house. I loved the rustic turquoise cast iron bench with Colorado river chair western cushions on it, standing in all its glory on their porch. I had a gorgeous view of beautiful daffodils right outside my bedroom window which Bruce had planted in springtime in their garden. Liz has a beautiful clothing shop, 'Little Bird' in Niwot town, and I have spent a lot of time browsing in her shop, buying beautiful dresses and listening to the great country music she would play, and I started to wear western clothing, and my dreams came true of when I was a little girl dreaming of one day to be a cowgirl! It really felt good to be me again. . .

Me and Liz would take walks together in the mind-blowing scenery of nature here in Colorado. I became interested in photography and hopefully, when you read this, I will have a book out with my photography.

I miss living next door to Liz and Bruce as it was a special time of us spending fun times together.

The Pioneer Inn

We would take drives up towards the mountains in Bruce's Mini Cooper convertible, enjoying the view of the mountains and the spectacular blue skies above us was magical. We drove up to Nederland which has a population of 1,400 people and was established in the nineteenth century as a trading post between Ute Indians and European settlers; the town's elevation is higher than 8,000 feet, and I used to feel very light-headed when I first used to go there. In 1874, the town was incorporated and adopted Nederland as the official name. It is interesting that the name of the town came from the Dutch Netherlands (means low land) and based on casual usage by Dutch miners in the 1850s.

I fell in love with Nederland; it was like going back in time to the seventies, full of hippies living in small houses, children running around freely with long hair, both boys and girls. I loved it. It also took me back to memories of when I visited Caribou Ranch in the seventies, which is very close by to Nederland town. I was married to Phil at the time, who was recording there. I'm still amazed of not knowing the that I would live nearby thirty-five years later and marry again.

The day I went with Liz and Bruce to Nederland, we decided to go to a restaurant in the town called The Pioneer Inn. We had the most delicious hamburgers and, falling into my dreams, I saw myself sitting at the bar all those years ago and one of the guys who worked at the Caribou Ranch was sitting next to me enjoying a beer with me and he carved my name, Jette, into the bar counter. Walking up to the bar which had never been replaced in these thirty-five years, my name 'Jette' was still visible in the old worn-out bar counter.

I was so much younger, and memories sitting by the bar wearing my little turquoise suede lace-up boots and pink dungarees and a short T-shirt saying 'Freedom' on the front. My hair was very long, right down to my waist, and on this day was tied up in a ponytail with a big purple ribbon. The Caribou guy next to me had his hair in a very long ponytail and had a big moustache and big heavy cowboy boots and a biker's black leather jacket with an eagle sewn onto the back. He had scruffy old faded blue jeans and a tight old T-shirt with a photo of the band The Rolling Stones on it.

The memories of The Pioneer Inn visualising the good times I had there thirty-five years before, now sitting around a table with my dear friends Liz and Bruce eating hamburgers, and nothing had changed, even the lighting of the booths along the walls was still the same, with all kinds of graffiti on the walls, and it really did feel that time was standing still. . .

CHAPTER 37

Twin Peaks

Life in Niwot became a very calm time for me, living in a small town. Walking down to town from the house I lived in took five minutes and I would start the day with a coffee at Mike and Patty's café, always meeting people I knew who all have become dear friends to me. I wrote a lot of words for my book in that café, listening to people's conversations, and there would be women sitting knitting in a corner talking about their husbands, which was very amusing to me. We would often be a crowd of people sitting out in front of the antique shop that Tim and Carrie owned, two shops away from the café, talking about the world, and having a bonfire in the evenings, sitting on their cast iron swings with a sheepskin covering our bodies on chilly nights, drinking too many beers. In the doorway of the Wise Buys antique shop, I would meet for the first time my now very dear friend, Joanne, where we started to talk about books. Through time, we started to take hikes together around the lakes, and to this day, we meet for coffees and have long chats about life.

My other friends, Joe and Cindi, who became close friends too, lived just down the road from me and they are a couple of hippies, living in a house with a 'Peace' sign on it, with their chickens, cats and a cute little dog, Moose, who's now sixteen years old. Each year, they have what they call a Moose festival for their dog's birthday. They have country bands playing in their garden, and you sit on haystacks and drink beers and have a dance while Joe will be making pizzas in the brick oven dome he built himself. Cindi made mosaic art on it out of beer bottles, and it looked beautiful.

I have had so many interesting conversations with Joe sitting at the Twin Peaks bar many times, having a beer. Not to mention the 'flying carpet' story we invented between us! It's a long story that Joe will giggle about if he reads my book. I had two of my birthdays celebrated in the restaurant. One of my birthday nights, I was handed a napkin by a woman with her phone number on it. Her name is Nancy and she and her husband, Bob, have now been my friends for six years. . . and Nancy was the one who would introduce me to James who I married many moons later. Sometimes the owner of the place would close up and lock the doors and he would put on old blues music, and we would all have a dance and sit at the bar until early morning while the kitchen chef would make pizzas for us all. It's such a small community of people in Niwot and I never in my dreams imagined, even if it was in my fantasies in my late teens, that I would live in a cowboy town one day, with houses with a swing on the porch and the sound of screen doors opening and closing was magic to me. All those dreams I had as a teenager would come true, having my own screen door in my own house many years later, just twenty minutes' drive away from Niwot here in Colorado.

Red Rocks

I remember the night me and my friends, Liz and Bruce, went to Red Rocks here in Colorado to see Tom Petty and The Heartbreakers in concert. Steve Ferrone, my friend, was the drummer in the band for many years before the tragedy happened, when Tom passed away in October 2017. The name of the band somehow relates to his death. It was to be Tom's last tour and he died a couple of months after I saw him play that night.

Joe Walsh started the show with the song 'Rocky Mountain Way' that he wrote when he lived in Boulder in the seventies, only twenty minutes away from where I live today. It wasn't until the late seventies that I visited Caribou Ranch where Joe Walsh recorded in the early seventies not knowing that into the eighties Phil would put together the 50th anniversary Fender guitar celebration show in London where Joe Walsh would be one of the artists playing that night.

I remember at the show, Tom looked very frail and was bending over his guitar like he was in pain, and he didn't walk very well when he was walking across the stage. It suddenly started to rain with thunder and lightning and the show was stopped for half an hour, and when they came back on stage, Tom had changed his jacket and I just remember that I felt something was not right with him. It was going to be his last tour before retiring to enjoy life with his family. I spoke to Steve on the phone from the bus they were on, heading back to their hotel, and I could hear Tom's very distinctive voice in the background, which kind of haunts me, thinking of him today.

CHAPTER 38

The White House

Going to the White House in Washington DC with Eric and his band was a very strange experience. We entered one of the back entrances through doors which had cameras which stripped off your clothes to see if you had any weapons on you. We were escorted through the office buildings to the back gardens where there was a helicopter ready to take George Bush Senior off the ground, and we were told to wave goodbye to him.

I was looking at these guys with rifles, sitting in the trees like birds watching every move we made, pointing the rifles at us. They had these evil bulldog faces and were ready to kill if you made a wrong move. I had an emerald-green cotton fabric dress on with a short jacket and brown suede zip-up ankle boots that were hurting my feet as they were brand new. I bent down to ease the pain by unzipping my boots as they were rubbing against my heels, and I heard that sound of a rifle being cocked, and I quickly stood up straight and felt the sweat running down my back in fear of what he was going to do next. He moved back behind a branch in the tree so he was difficult to see, and I took a deep breath and looked straight ahead, watching Bush taking off. I was holding Phil's hand and I was shaking all over.

I remember as I was walking through the office building there was a big heavy solid mahogany desk standing to the left of the room with the surface of the desk filled with phones ringing at the same time, and the woman who was in charge of receiving the millions of calls through the day looked bewildered trying to answer each call. As we left the building, walking through the hallway to the exit door, I realised that my dress was clinging to my body with sweat as I had just been through a very frightening and disturbing experience to be behind closed doors at the White House on a very warm day.

CHAPTER 39

Ray Cooper's Rituals

In 1990, I went to the big concert at Knebworth House in England. I was so excited to see Phil playing on stage with the house band, and Eric Clapton, Mark Knopfler and Elton John were all on stage together.

I remember watching Ray Cooper, the percussionist, going backstage, carrying his suit over his arm and hanging it up on the door of the dressing room. He would sit down in his tracksuit and get a cigar out and he would light it and the divine smell of the cigar would fill the room with a haze of smoke, creating an atmosphere of excitement for the big show to come on in a few hours. He would get a bandage out to wrap around each finger, very precisely and slowly covering each finger so it wouldn't hurt when he started to play. I was fascinated, watching him hyping himself up, slowly taking his tracksuit off while he puffed on his cigar and put on his very 1950's vintage linen suit which had wide pleated legs and tapered ankles. Just before he got up on stage, he would walk up and down, making deep humming sounds, hyping himself up to jump up on stage. He would put his little round dark glasses on just before he got on stage. It was amazing to see how he became someone else at that moment in time, and when he hit those percussions with his fingers wrapped in bandages, magic happened and his playing gave me the goosebumps down my spine.

Meeting Celebrities

The day before the concert I had gone out and bought myself a new dress. It was a long, floral V-neck gypsy dress with a sweeping full skirt, and when I put it on, it clung nicely to my body. I put on my old brown suede seventies knee boots which still fitted my slender legs, and the old wool felt floppy hat with feathers around the brim was a must to wear. I took a taxi to the Knebworth grounds and met my Phil at the back of the stage. I took photos of Eric and the band, all in their Gianni Versace suits. Eric's suit was pale pink, and his hair was long. When he started to play 'Cocaine', his left foot would be dancing from side to side. It always amused me to see what made him get into those movements when he started to play his guitar. Mark Knopfler of Dire Straits had a rusty yellow colour suit on, and as always was wearing his cowboy boots, and when he started to play *Money for Nothing*, I felt like dancing.

As it happened, I was at the front of the stage, and Princess Margaret's son, David Armstrong (Viscount Linley), was standing next to me, and he said, 'Would you like to dance?' I said that I would love to. He put his arms around me and asked me if I lived in the town. I told him I used to live not far from Knebworth town years before, but now I was living in France with my husband, Phil, the guitarist in the band.

He smiled and said, 'I like your husband's playing,' and we ended by saying to each other, 'Nice talking to you,' and we both blended back into the big crowd of people around us.

I thought I would never see him again, but I did twelve years later, at The Golden Jubilee Concert for his aunt the Queen. Elton John was walking around backstage waiting to get on stage, and as I walked past him, he stopped me and asked, 'Are you with the band?'

'No, I'm not, but I'm married to the guitarist in the band,' I told him. I noticed he had an earring in his right ear, and I asked him: 'Is that a feather you have in your ear?'

'Yes, it is,' he said, 'I was given the earring from a friend who told me it will protect me from illness and give me a long life.'

'Can I touch it for luck?' I asked, and he said, 'Please do.'

He then went back up on stage and started to play 'Sacrifice'. Phil went on stage wearing a deep blue Versace suit and he was over the moon to be playing with these three amazing musicians.

Steve Ferrone

Steve Ferrone, the drummer in Eric's band at the time, became a close friend to me, and it's a small world as he was born back in Brighton in England; funny to think that my youngest son, Charlie, would be studying medicine at Brighton University, close to where Steve was born.

Steve and I met up after many years of not seeing each other. We were walking on the Brighton Palace Pier on the south coast of England, and he said to me: 'I used to play here on the pier with my friends when I was a little boy. I loved the doughnuts they sold here, and I used to hang out at the fairground. I also did tap dance classes in the town when I was in my teens.'

'How I would have loved to see you do tap dancing!' I said. He told me many fun stories of his life in Brighton. We sat on the beach having an ice cream and he smoked one of his

Havana cigars which I love the smell of, and that night he introduced me to the best fish and chips in town. He has a very distinctive laugh which was very charming to me, and still is. He has been living in LA for years, and it's interesting that many moons later, I now live in the US too.

CHAPTER 40

Four Seasons Hotel

In 1991, Phil had a call from the office of Mark Knopfler, asking if he would like to join Dire Straits' upcoming world tour. And he said, 'Yes I'd love to.'

During that world tour, I travelled with my oldest son, who was seven at the time, to Los Angeles to meet up with Phil. We were staying at the Four Seasons Hotel and one night I wrapped our son Oliver in a warm coat and put on my long blue cotton bohemian coat with wildflowers all over it. I loved that coat.

I put on my brown suede knee-high boots which died on me not long after our return home from the tour. I never found a pair again which was so soft; they more or less hung over my ankles at the end of their life.

It was a chilly night, and I held my son's hand tight as we walked to a food store which was only five minutes from the hotel. The police drove by us, and they rolled the window down, asking me why I was walking as it was too dangerous to walk around at night. I was in shock as it was the first time I had felt danger in Los Angeles! We turned around and went back to the hotel, and never got to the store.

My first encounter with Mark Knopfler was in the hallway of the hotel. Me and my son were walking back to our room. He looked kind of lonely; he was wearing his cap back to front, and his shoulders were bent and he walked at a very slow pace. He said 'Hi' to Oliver and asked him if he wanted to come up to his room to play with his twin boys who were the same age as my son. I looked at my son who looked a little bewildered, but he took his hand and went off to play in Mark's room.

Through the days being around the band, I watched Mark behind the stage. He had a long mirror in his changing room, and his private assistant would put the headband on his head just before he walked on stage. I would watch his saxophone player, Chris, behind the stage, polishing his saxophones one by one. They were so shiny I could see myself in each one of them. He had little boxes lined up with a different pair of cowboy boots in each box which he also polished for hours! I took Oliver to see the concert in Los Angeles and we went backstage, passing the boxes. I took out one pair of cowboy boots and put my son inside the box and took a photo of him. Chris was not amused but I love the photo of my son in the box to this day, as it gives me memories of the time we toured with Dire Straits.

Limousine Chat

I remember one night in Rome after the concert was over and we were going back to the hotel. It was an outdoor concert, and I was sitting in a limousine behind the stage waiting for the band to come off stage. I had a chat with the driver while waiting and he told me he had a loving wife and two children who were watching the concert and he had been a fan of Dire Straits for many years. It was interesting to look at his face in the rear-view mirror as he had a headband on his head and a jacket which said Dire Straits on it, which he had been given by one of the roadies. He asked me what band member I was married to, and I said the electric guitarist, Phil Palmer. He asked me if it was hard being married to a musician. I wrapped my suede jacket tight around me, somehow feeling cold, as I felt the trauma of being in the rock and roll world wasn't a healthy place for me to be.

I fell into my dreamy memories of when me and Phil were walking hand in hand after I had finished my English lesson at college when I was still an au pair for his Uncle Dave. I remember coming out of the college door and he was standing there in his too-small blue army coat and his red Kickers shoes with holes in them. His long curly hair was hanging over his shoulders and he looked right at me with his loving brown eyes, and I fell in love with him there and then.

I fell out of my dreams and looked at the driver looking at me in the back mirror, waiting for me to answer his question, but I never did as I didn't know the answer. I was more interested and fascinated by all the bottles of wine and sandwiches which were in a glass cabinet in front of me where I sat on the back seat, waiting for Phil to sit next to me.

I watched the band coming off stage looking very sweaty, and one of the assistants was wrapping each band member in a blue dressing gown, so they didn't get a chill. It was like a dream to me, how much life had changed, seeing my hippie boyfriend now in a blue dressing gown, jumping into the limousine and complaining why there were no ham sandwiches while we drove off with a police escort in front and behind us.

Pink Panther

Life became very lonely for me as time went by; I didn't like the show business world we now seemed to live in. I remember one night we were having dinner at the hotel with the band, and I had got a babysitter for my son. She was Chinese and couldn't speak much English. I felt a little worried for Oliver as I gave him a goodnight kiss and he just looked at me with sad eyes as I turned around and walked out of the hotel room. The hotel corridors seemed to go on forever with the same boring grey wool carpets which I really started to dislike. I counted the circle pattern in the carpet as I got nearer the lift to go down four floors to the dining area. I looked at myself in the mirror in the lift and I thought I didn't look happy.

I had my hair up in a ponytail with a flower in it that I had picked from a vase of flowers in the hotel room we were in. I had a beautiful blue silk dress on and, of course, my old suede knee boots. I walked into the dining room where the band was sitting around the table, and I sat myself down next to Phil. I was talking to the percussion player, Danny, who was sitting across the table from me and we talked about his children and how much he missed them. As we were talking, I looked over to the staircase next to the lift area and Oliver was standing on the last step walking into the hall area in his little striped pyjamas with his Pink Panther under his arm, running to me barefoot. He was crying and told me the babysitter was asleep on the bed upstairs. He must have walked all four floors down on the staircase!

I hugged him tight and put him on his dad's lap. I went upstairs to the room where I found the babysitter sleeping on the bed next to a swan she had made out of a bath towel. I woke her up and told her to leave as I was not happy with her.

I wrapped myself in a warm coat as I felt chilled thinking of what could have happened to him, and walked slowly down the stairs thinking of what had happened to Eric's son, Conor. I wrapped my son in a warm blanket and held him tight for the rest of the evening.

CHAPTER 41

Joan Armatrading

Phil went on a tour with Joan Armatrading in the early seventies. I remember sitting on the bus they were touring in, next to Joan. She was wearing a bohemian-style blue striped shirt and black jeans. I loved the silver bracelet she was wearing which had a turquoise heart-shaped stone in it. We talked about the turquoise stone and what it stands for: water and sky, health and protection. I loved her cute puff ball hairstyle and we would sit a little later at a restaurant talking of her childhood in Saint Kitts. Her partner was a really nice lady, and we had a wonderful evening laughing and enjoyed a bit of normality before she became famous, when things always change. Little did I know that I would visit the island of Saint Kitts many moons later in my life, and I would visit where she was born and think back on a peaceful conversation with her on a bus ride. . .

CHAPTER 42

Tina Turner

Phil did a tour with Tina Turner in 1989. I remember the concert when Phil had to do a wiggle-wiggle with Tina, holding her around the waist, to the song 'Nutbush City Limits'. He hated doing that every night especially as the roadies would stand at the side of the stage, giving him points with cards held up in the air, and me standing next to them having a laugh at the entertainment that was going on.

One day I was sitting on the tour bus right at the back. I was talking to the drummer of the band, and he was a very interesting man. I was in my tight brown velour trousers and my beloved suede cowboy boots which were falling apart. My hair was up in a ponytail with an embossed red floral ribbon I had kept from a bouquet of roses my mother had sent me for my birthday. I loved my red floral cotton fabric top which I had worn a thousand times, but always felt so good in. As we started a conversation across the aisle of the bus seats, I was amazed by his outfit. When I saw him playing on stage, he had massive muscles with many tattoos, and wore a white sleeveless vest and a pair of very tight jeans.

Looking at him now after the concert was over, driving along on the bus back to the hotel, he was wearing a floral dress and high-heeled shoes. His toy monkey, occupying the seat next to him, was also wearing a floral dress the same as his. We had a conversation about cross-dressing and he told me he had all his women's clothing specially made for his rather large body. I was fascinated by his stories and we had a laugh about what people might think of him. I gave him a kiss on the cheek and said to him, 'You are you, that is all that matters.' As he dozed off with his monkey in his arms, I looked over my seat and I could see Tina Turner's bald head poking up over the top of the seat without her famously spiky hair wig on. I walked down the aisle of the bus and sat behind her. I was thinking of Ike Turner, of the cruelty of mental and physical abuse she went through with him. . . little did I know that our very short conversation would come back to me after my long, unfulfilling marriage sadly came to an end after Phil's affairs, lies, and mental abuse. The rock and roll life can be very harmful, and you have to pay a price for being an entertainer and still hold on to your sanity in the real world outside the stage performances. I saw for myself through the rock and roll years so many marriages falling apart.

CHAPTER 43

George Michael

George Michael's world tour was the final chapter for me and Phil, and our marriage was over by 2010 after thirty-two years. George was a kind man, and I had the privilege of talking to him once briefly as he came off stage. It was a very strange experience as I sat backstage with my youngest son Charlie on two high chairs by a little bar.

George walked with a surreal silence through the room to where his assistant was ready to undress him. He put a track-suit on and a cap, then he was ready to fly back to his house in North London. He came and sat near me on a bar stool waiting to be called out to his private helicopter, and he looked bewildered into my eyes.

He asked me who I was as he had never met me before. I told him I was the wife of his guitarist and he looked confused as he had only ever seen Phil with his mistress. We talked for a moment, while we could hear the crowd shouting his name out in the concert hall. He had sweat running down his neck and his hands were deep in his pockets. He said to me that he was glad the concert was over, and I should take good care of myself and my son. Then he was called out to the helicopter, and it was like he was an angel who came to me in that room that night and made me realise what was going on behind my back. I never saw Michael again. . .

CHAPTER 44

Buckingham Palace

On the 3rd of June in 2002, I was in a limousine driving to Buckingham Palace, the largest private garden in London. The driver asked me, 'Are you an artist performing on the stage tonight?' I said no, I was the wife of the guitarist playing in the house band.

I had been invited to 'The Party at the Palace'. It was a celebration of the Queen's Golden Jubilee. I looked at myself in the driver's rear-view mirror, thinking that I looked a million dollars in my original Biba black lace over beige satin full maxi dress, along with my old brown suede boots and the old felt hat with feathers around the brim. I was looking at my vintage Biba feather handbag which was lying on the seat next to me. It had the invitation card from the Queen inside the bag. It had gold-edges around it and I was holding on tight to the bag with my very dark red polished nails looking shiny on my hands, and my long hair hanging over my shoulders.

The driver was keen to chat as I could see he kept looking at me in the rear-view mirror. 'Have you got children?' he asked.

I said, 'Yes, I have two boys. Have you got children?'

'Yes', he replied, 'my two boys are working here tonight at the security entrance.'

I said, 'Perhaps I will meet them at the entrance. What are their names?'

'It's Ben and Steve,' he told me.

I felt I wanted to be quiet, and I was looking out of the window thinking how surreal it was to be driving up the path of the Queen's gardens. I looked out of the window, sitting a long way away from the driver in this vast limousine, feeling kind of lonely. I saw security men standing by the trees all the way up to the back of the stage. There were security cameras hanging from the tree branches, which looked out of place in these beautiful pink blossomed English hawthorn trees. I asked the driver if we could stop the car so I could pick a flower to put in my hat. He didn't answer as we were coming up to the back of the stage. I said goodbye to him, and we hugged, and he said, 'Take good care of yourself.' I wondered why he was saying that. Perhaps he could see I felt lonely and a little lost in this environment of the rock and roll world.

Phil was standing at the backstage door, and we hugged, and he took me to my seat and the show began. One of the acts was Phil's uncle, Ray Davies, who was playing 'Waterloo Sunset' and I reflected on how I ended up here, being a member of the Davies and Palmer family. Thinking back to when I was sixteen living in Denmark, and my boyfriend, Vagn, buying me The Kinks album, *Kinks*, and I would move to London seven years later and marry the nephew of Ray Davies.

The show was filled with talented artists, and I enjoyed sitting in my seat close to the stage, drinking champagne and being entertained on a beautiful warm summer night. I met most of the artists at the after-party at the Queen's house, which was another surreal moment. Phil and I were holding hands walking up the path leading to the Palace. . . it was a beautiful path, surrounded by gorgeous rose bushes smelling divine, and there was a full moon. We were walking behind Ozzie Osbourne from Black Sabbath and Brian Wilson from the Beach Boys.

Ozzie had dyed pink hair at the front of his long black hair, and he had his famous round John Lennon glasses on with a pink tint in them. He was wearing a black suit and a chunky silver chain with a big cross hanging over his chest, and he had his arm around Brian Wilson's shoulder, who somehow looked plain in his outfit of a grey suit and white shirt and blue tie. I was mesmerised by Ozzie's tattoos all the way up his arm, and he was clinging to Brian Wilson, and put his fingers through Brian's grey hair. He said to Brian, 'You are more nuts than I am!' They both laughed at each other, and Sharon Osbourne (Ozzie's wife) holding on to Ozzie's arm was also laughing, which amused me as her laughter was very distinctive.

We entered Buckingham Palace at the east front wing which was built in 1703 for the Duke of Buckingham and has 775 rooms. I walked up the very wide cream and gold-coloured staircase, with thick red wool carpet which somehow clung to my boots. I had to take two steps at a time to get to the top of the vast landing and we walked into a room furnished with regency-style Chinese furniture.

As we entered the room, I was looking around and saw all these familiar celebrities' faces and I felt so intrigued to be walking around talking to them all. I was suddenly faced by Tony Blair (the Prime Minister at the time) and all I could think of saying to him was, 'You used to have long hair when you were in a rock and roll band!'

He laughed and said, 'Yes I did, when I was a student.'

'What was your band called?' I asked.

He told me they were called 'Ugly Rumours', and his idol was Mick Jagger and his desire was to be a rock star. 'I rebelled at having my hair cut four times a term at university,' he told me, 'and so I had what I called a tick, tick, tick, tick four-days-in-a-row haircut. I was told by the headmaster that I should have a haircut, and I told him that I'd had all four already!'

We laughed and I looked around and saw Phil talking to Paul McCartney and Olivia Harrison, who had lost George the year before to cancer. She looked beautiful in her black velvet dress, and her stunning brown eyes mesmerised me. We talked for a little while, and I could tell through our conversation that it hadn't been an easy ride being married to George, and I felt I could relate to her story with my own situation in a rock and roll marriage. Her voice was very soothing, and she said to me 'Take good care of yourself,' which was the second time I was told that on that night. . . must have meant something for me to think about, as I realised it did many years later.

I said, 'You too, it was nice to meet you.'

I started to talk to Paul McCartney standing next to Olivia. I asked him did he ever miss his hometown, Liverpool, where it all started for him as a young boy. He said, 'I do miss the good times I had with my dad when me and John played songs for him in the living room. We were playing, "She loves you, yeah, yeah, yeah" for him, and my dad said, "It sounds okay, but put 'yes, yes, yes' instead of 'yeah, yeah, yeah' as it sounds too American."'

We giggled and I said, 'What a lovely memory and story.' Phil would be playing with Paul McCartney numerous times over the coming years.

The room was full of familiar faces from Tom Jones, Elton John, Rod Stewart, Steve Winwood, Shirley Bassey, Bryan Adams and many more. I had a small chat with Prince Charles and Camilla who asked me what I did for a living. I told them I had a full-time job being a wife and a mother. They looked kind of bewildered and walked away. We were told that the Queen had gone to bed before the concert was over - I'm sure with her three Pembroke Welsh Corgi dogs. That was the end of a very surreal evening. As me and Phil drove home, we were both thinking, *Were we dreaming or was this evening a real event?*

I had a big surprise when I opened the front door to our house. Our dog Smokie had locked herself into a room while we were out, and she had peed in all my shoes! I spent the rest of the evening on my knees cleaning up after Smokie and scrubbing the floor.

Somehow the surreal evening among celebrities vanished into the night.

CHAPTER 45

The Strat Pack Live Concert

I remember a brief moment in time in 2004, when I was driving to Wembley Arena in London to see The Strat Pack Live in Concert for the 50th anniversary of the Fender Stratocaster, which Phil had put together.

I arrived backstage and I felt good in a pair of Levis and a short white off-the-shoulder top and my old brown suede boots. I had my long hair loose over my shoulders with a pink rose behind my right ear that smelled divinely of summertime. I always wanted to have a tattoo of a butterfly on top of my right shoulder one day as a sign of freedom, as I had started to feel stronger and wanted to find out who I was as me, Jette. I never had the tattoo until after my divorce seven years later.

I sat in the front row and fell into my dreams when the show started.

Brian May from Queen came on stage, wearing a multi-coloured shirt and with a brown and white Fender guitar in front of him. I remembered him two years earlier, standing on the rooftop of Buckingham Palace at the Golden Jubilee playing a solo of the British National Anthem. It was a windy day, and his long curly hair was blowing in the wind, quite a sight you would never see again.

Hank Marvin came on stage in a black suit with a red Fender hanging in front of him. He had his big glasses on that we all remember him for from the time he was the lead guitarist in The Shadows, and he played *Sleepwalk*. . . it was like a dream with his very special smooth sound on his guitar, as he really is a Stratocaster legend. The song made me fall into my dreams of the Caribbean Sea in Barbados. I would be swimming in the turquoise sea which felt like silk on my body, and I was thinking of the moment of Hank's smooth guitar playing.

Paul Carrack, who has beautiful voice, came on playing *How Long* in his funny little black hat. It had a red star in the middle and he had a striped shirt on which matched his cream Fender guitar. I love that song as it gives me so many lovely memories, and Phil played on the track. The song took me back to my and Paul's conversation at a producer's house. He said to me, 'I believe strongly in being a family man and I have four beautiful children and a beautiful wife.'

I said, 'How lovely. . . you know I'm married to Phil your guitarist?' I will always remember the words he said to me.

'It seems difficult for some musicians to be faithful to their wives in this profession, as perhaps being away from family for months at a time can be a sacrifice you make.' All these little hints through time made me question my marriage as I found out later in life. . .

David Gilmour came on in his beautiful blue silk shirt and black trousers, carrying a white Fender over his shoulder, playing *Coming Back to Life*. I went into another dream world with his beautiful distinctive guitar sound.

How amazing that I would see him fourteen years later, sitting next to me and my husband-to-be James in a restaurant on Hydra Island in Greece on a beautiful summer night, and the beauty of his face from when he was young was still there in his eyes.

So many amazing artists were playing that night: Joe Walsh, Albert Lee, Mike Rutherford, Ronnie Wood and more. . . It was a night to remember and Phil, who was in the house band all through the night, played his Fenders as he has his own style which is a very mellow sound of the guitar to me.

It was a night to remember, along with all the other moments in time of being around the beauty of very talented musicians over the previous thirty years, before my marriage ended in 2010.

CHAPTER 46

Moving to the South of France

Me and Phil decided to move to France with our young son Oliver while Phil was touring with Eric Clapton. We rented a small house up in the hills a little away from Cap d'Antibes on the south coast. We were tired after the long trip driving to France, and I put Oliver's suitcases in his room, and we opened all the white painted shutters, and we all sat watching the sunset over the beautiful view of the mountains. I had bought olives and a baguette and cheeses at the marketplace in Antibes on our way up to the house, and after a warm shower, I wrapped Oliver and myself into the patchwork quilt my grandmother had made me. We said our goodbyes to Phil as he had to leave to join Eric's tour starting in Italy.

I will always remember that moment in time, the first night in a new country, lying next to Oliver listening to him breathing in and out, short warm breaths of air against my cheeks, and hearing the new chirping sound of crickets (I read once that the male crickets are rubbing their legs against each other making the chirping sound). It was a very soothing sound and we fell into our dreams. I hugged Oliver tight as he lay on my chest, and as my heart was beating against his face, his head moved peacefully from side to side. I gently lifted him away from me and put him next to me on the bed with his favourite Pink Panther wrapped around his right arm.

The Moody Blues

Miracles seemed to happen in that beautiful little house up on the hill, as I gave birth to beautiful Charlie a year later.

I remember when Charlie was newborn, Justin Hayward from The Moody Blues, who lived nearby, came for a visit at the little house. He sat down on the old worn-out provincial antique couch, looking like a mirror of the past when he was very young, with his blond hair and blue eyes and his beautiful distinctive voice when he sang 'Nights in White Satin' and I fell into my dreams of listening to The Moody Blues when I was seventeen at my first boyfriend Jan's house. Jan never went to school after he heard the sound of the Moody Blues. He would sit in his room all day listening to their songs and smoking pot. And here was Justin sitting on my couch twenty-five years later with my baby Charlie in his lap.

During the time we lived in France, Phil co-produced an album with Justin, *The View from the Hill*. It fascinates me how my life became more and more like a jigsaw puzzle with so many pieces finding their way into the right places and becoming a piece of art, full of synchronised moments of finding the right paths along the never-ending road for me. . .

CHAPTER 47

Gauloises Cigarettes

After a bad experience of being bullied by other children in a local French school, I moved Oliver to an English-speaking school in a pretty little hilltop town called Mougins. I remember driving to the school in my soft top convertible black VW Golf, which had a steering wheel made of walnut wood. I loved that car, and I was taken by the beauty of the pine, olive, and cypress trees and many restaurants surrounding the medieval streets arranged in a circle in Mougins village.

I would kiss my son Oliver on his cheeks and promise I would be back soon to pick him up. I could see him in my rearview mirror waving to me, as he took the teacher's hand and turned around. His school bag dragged on the ground, and his long hair waved from side to side in the very warm breeze as he walked quickly up the stairs, still holding on to the teacher's hand. I felt like turning around and hugging him one more time before he disappeared into the school building.

I would pick him up late afternoon, after I had taken a drive to Cannes to play tennis with my tennis coach. It was a hot day and while we were playing the game, she suddenly said,

'*Un moment s'il vous plaît!*' We stopped playing, and I walked over to get my bottle of water and dried my neck with a white towel which had a hand-sewn pink rose on it which my mother had given me. It had been with me in my suitcase travelling the world ever since I started to travel. I looked at my coach and she was lighting a cigarette, and I was amazed how she could play tennis and smoke a cigarette at the same time. I thought to myself 'Welcome to France!' as it is a land of people who smoke the very strong Gauloises. . .

Mel Gibson

After Oliver got used to the school and liked going there, and seeing him finding friends, I would take French lessons at the school twice a week.

I remember sitting down at my desk one day, taking out my French books, and I looked up at a man asking me if he could sit next to me at the desk which was a two-seater. He looked familiar. He was not very tall and he had very deep blue eyes which were hypnotising, and I had to look away, but I realised that he was the actor, Mel Gibson.

We would talk after lessons in the school yard. He told me he was acting in a movie being filmed in the south of France for six months and he had moved his wife, Robyn, and his eight children to France who all went to the school, and in Oliver's class, there were two of his boys. I told him I really liked the movie he was in, *The Man Without a Face* which, funny enough, he directed too! The film is based on Isabelle Holland's 1972 novel of the same name.

I never saw his wife as he always picked up his children after school hours. After six months doing French lessons in the same classroom and having chats in the school yard, I never saw Mel Gibson again.

CHAPTER 48

The Man on a White Horse

I used to hike in the beautiful mountains close to the small town of Gourdon situated in the southeast region of France. Gourdon is the capital of the Bouriane, which extends up to the Dordogne River.

On a warm summer day me and eight other mothers from the school packed our rucksacks with sandwiches, water and a small bottle of champagne, as it was one of the mothers' birthdays, and we wanted to celebrate with the champagne when we reached the top of the mountain three hours later. I had bought a pair of sunglasses with suede material on the sides, as the sun was so bright hiking up the mountains, and it felt magical looking out of my glasses, seeing the view overlooking the Dordogne River in a light I can't describe other than breathtaking. When we got to the top of the mountain, I took my featherweight pastel green jacket off, and it was heavenly feeling the mountain breeze air through my Scotch plaid flannel shirt, touching my skin and cooling me down. My legs were bathed in sunshine from my knees down to my ankles, where my feet were covered in a pair of Canyonlands walking boots. I sat myself down in a field full of tiny wild mountain bee orchids which had the most breathtaking purple and pink colours wrapped around each other like a velvet carpet. I and the other mothers laid ourselves down in the middle of the magic of the scenery of the orchids and decided to open our bottles of champagne.

I asked the birthday girl if she had any wishes as it was her fortieth birthday. She told me she wished for a handsome man riding on a white horse to pass us women lying there sunbathing on top of the world, a thousand feet above the clouds! I looked around and there he was! I can't explain that moment of magic but it's the real truth of what happened in that moment in time. He was the most beautiful man I have ever seen, riding his white horse without a saddle, and his body shone with beauty, half-covered by a sheepskin rug over his shoulders. He had fully quilled, handmade native American regalia moccasins and a porcupine quilled beaded dragonfly neck pouch around his neck on his bare chest, and his black hair was tied back in a ponytail, hanging down to his waist. The birthday girl sat up in amusement with an open mouth, as she couldn't believe what she saw, as much as he couldn't believe these eight women all over him, not knowing that the little stone house right behind where we were sitting was his home.

He told us we were welcome to come up to see where he lived. We walked up with our champagne bottles in our hands and sat down in front of the door into his little stone house. The doorframe was draped with a sheep skin and he had sheep grazing in the fields among the wild orchids, and we all just couldn't believe this dream was for real. He told us his name was Achak which means 'spirit', and he had lived in his stone house for fifteen years, after he left the civilisation of the town where he was born in the north of France. He told us he couldn't imagine living any other way than with his sheep and the peaceful mountains surrounding him.

We said our goodbyes and finished our champagne, and it was time to walk down the mountain. Somehow we were all in a daze – was this a dream we had just experienced? Or was it real?

When we got into our cars to drive back to the school to pick up our children, I felt I had been on another planet for the day, full of freedom and thoughts of what it really is all about, being a human being. Oliver came running towards me, and I hugged him tight, telling him that I had a beautiful bedtime story to tell him when I tucked him into bed that evening.

I never saw Achak again.

CHAPTER 49

Gary Moore

I was driving home after tennis along the French Riviera, passing the famous Palais des Festivals where they hold the Festival de Cannes. I was wearing my baby-blue tracksuit and trainers, and I had the soft top down on my car, and stopped the car to take my tracksuit top off as I felt very warm after the game of tennis. I looked in the rear-view mirror of the car, and I saw the guitarist, Gary Moore, walking along on the pavement with his guitar hung over his shoulder. I often saw him in a playground in Juan-Les-Pins close to where I lived in Antibes. Our children would play together while we were sitting on a bench talking about the music world. He was an amazing guitarist and he told me stories of his life and who he had played with over the years.

In his youth he had joined the band Thin Lizzy with Phil Lynott in the sixties back in England. I asked him if he had played in a club called Dingwalls in north London. He said yes, he had, and I told him that I used to go to Dingwalls with my friend, Annie, in the late seventies, watching bands playing there and getting a little drunk; Annie would end up in the toilets after too many glasses of wine, and I wouldn't see her for hours. He laughed and said, 'Yes, they were the good old days.' When I play his song, 'Still got the Blues', it gives me the shivers to hear his guitar playing and I think of those moments sitting on a bench in Juan-Les-Pins back in France having a chat with him. And sometimes I feel sad he's here no more.

Smokie

Coming out of my thoughts of Gary Moore, I was driving up the hill to the school, and I saw Oliver standing outside the school holding his teacher's hand. She asked me if she could talk to me for a moment as she had been talking to Oliver about liking dogs.

She told me her dog, Ella, had had twelve puppies, and she hoped people would take a puppy from her as she lived in a small apartment and they were driving her crazy. Oliver looked at me with his beautiful big green eyes, and asked me if we should go and see the puppies. I took his hand and strapped him in the seat belt in the back seat of the car, and off we went to see the puppies.

We walked twenty steps up to the apartment on the second floor, and the teacher opened the door. We walked into her living room, and poor Ella was lying on the floor feeding the puppies as best as she could. It was like being in the movie *101 Dalmatians*; there were puppies everywhere, and a few of them escaped to the kitchen area. I took my son's hand and we walked into the kitchen, where there were three puppies lying on top of each other. I left Oliver in the kitchen to choose one of them and when he came out I went in to make my choice. I looked at a little furry, white-coated puppy with three black spots on her back and one brown spot on her tail. She looked so cute, and I asked Oliver to come into the kitchen and tell me which one he liked. It turned out that we chose the same puppy, and as we drove home in my car with our puppy, we decided to call her Smokie!

She lived a long life and I felt at the time she had something to do with me feeling maternal again as I was pregnant with beautiful Charlie the same year we got Smokie in 1993.

CHAPTER 50

Sonny

Charlie was born pretty much nine months later in January 1994, in a hospital in Grasse, the world capital of perfume. Grasse has had a prospering perfume industry since the end of the 18th century. The jasmine flower is the key ingredient of many perfumes, and one of them is the famous Chanel No 5. Grasse produces over two-thirds of France's natural aromas for perfume and for food flavourings.

I was telling my dear friend, Sonny, who was our gardener at our house, that it was time to take me to the hospital as my waters had broken. Phil was back in England working with Roger Daltrey (from The Who) and never came in time to see me giving birth to Charlie.

I was sitting in the back of Sonny's old car, swaying from side to side as we drove along the winding mountain roads overlooking the fields covered in jasmine flowers; the smell coming through the car windows was overpowering. I fell into my dreams of lying in the jasmine fields while I was counting how many minutes there were between my contractions, while Sonny was talking to me of his family back in Thailand and how he missed them, and I just wanted to tell him to be quiet. I felt very hot in my pale blue cotton linen midi dress, which had little pockets on it. I put my hands into each pocket so I could feel my big round football-shaped stomach tightening as the baby moved around, ready to see the world.

I had a broad-brimmed straw hat on my head with a turquoise leather string around the brim which hung over the hat at the back, and I could feel it against my sweaty neck. The warm sun was shining through the car window into my eyes. I was wearing my big round black-framed sunglasses, which had pale pink lenses in them, but the light from the sun still felt so bright. I closed my eyes while I could hear Sonny talking to me, and the sound of his voice became more and more distant as I was still holding onto my baby, whispering to him, 'It won't be long before you will see the world as I do through my eyes.'

We arrived at the hospital after a bumpy ride over the dirt roads and narrow, sharp bends, which had made me feel a little car sick on top of the contractions. . .

Sonny helped me out of the car as I felt the contractions were getting stronger and stronger, and I took very slow steps up to the big iron gate, where Sonny pulled the big, heavy, metal chain and the sound of the bell rang in my ears.

A very big woman with a very big bust appeared. She was dressed in her black-and-white tunic outfit called a habit, and she looked like a nun. She had a crucifix hanging on a long chain over her chest which she was holding onto with her big hands, which blinded me as it flashed in the reflection of the sun. She opened the gate. I felt fearful looking into her eyes after I said my goodbyes to Sonny, but I was in so much pain that I just followed her into the room where I waited to be seen by the doctor.

He came into the room to talk to me, and I started to feel calm, as I liked him. He had a kind face and a lovely smile. His black hair came down to his shoulders. I tried to say through my eyes that I wasn't happy being here in this hospital run by nuns. He seemed to understand how I felt and gave me a hug and told me everything was going to be okay.

After being checked over, he told me that my baby was in distress with an irregular heartbeat, and he would do a caesarean in a couple of hours' time. By then, my dear friend, Joanna, had arrived and sat herself next to me, trying to calm me down. She told me that I should stop talking and rest, as I was talking nonsense out of pure fear of knowing that I was giving birth to my baby in two hours. It did make me laugh what Joanna said to me, and I was thinking of how we had both lived next door to each other in England, many years before we were married, and before she left for her travels around the world. And now we were meeting up again in France, after so many moons passing. Being pregnant with my second child at the same time as Joanna was having her third was so beautiful; I loved spending time with her through our pregnancies, and to this day we still keep in touch, even though I live in Colorado and she lives in England. Hopefully our lives will cross each other's paths again one day.

CHAPTER 51

Baby Charlie

Phil and Oliver arrived from England to see the new baby, Charlie. I kissed and hugged them both. It was so good to see them, and I was holding Oliver tight and told him I would see him soon back home at the house in a couple of days. He looked at me straight in the eyes with a few tears running down his cheeks as he would rather stay with me than fly back to England. I wiped his tears from his cheeks and said to him, 'Do you want to hold your little brother?' He said yes and I wrapped Charlie in the pale blue linen blanket my mother had given me as a present for him. I gently put Charlie into Oliver's arms and looked at both of them through my eyes, and it was a picture I have treasured in my mind and heart forever.

I kissed Oliver on his cheeks, which still felt wet on my lips from the tears, and he kissed his baby brother on his forehead then we said our goodbyes. I hugged them both and that evening they had to fly back to London.

Baby Blues

I felt lonely in this convent of a hospital, which was a very gloomy place, and my room was so plain and dark with one bright light hanging from the ceiling. The doctor who had delivered Charlie came into the room, asking me how I was doing. I told him that I felt I had the baby blues, not being able to hold my baby as I was hooked up with tubes hanging from everywhere on my body. I asked him if he could give me my baby who was lying next to me in his little baby crib which had clear glass around it, and I could see him through it, looking at me with his big blue eyes. I couldn't see his hands and tiny feet as Phil had wrapped him in the pale blue linen blanket again before he put him down in the crib, before the goodbyes, and I had watched him and Oliver disappear through the door like a breeze of wind blew them away from me.

The doctor picked him up and put him in my arms, and my baby felt warm against my body. I put him to my breast and he took to my milk straight away. I unwrapped him so he could put his hands against my skin, and he smelled so divine and his quick breathing against my breast felt so soothing to me. We were bonding into our own little bubble, the second time around of motherhood.

Les Oranges

Shortly after Charlie was born, we moved to a bigger house on the coastline of Antibes which was called 'Les Oranges'. It was a beautiful old Victorian house with the overwhelming fragrance of a spectacular blue moon Wisteria Vine hanging all over the white painted front wall of the house. All the windows in the house had pale blue wooden shutters.

I would wake up early on a warm spring day, wrapping myself into my long red silk Japanese vintage kimono, checking my boys if they were still sleeping, and I would walk down barefoot on the ceramic lemon-coloured tiled staircase which felt cooling underneath my feet. My little Indian gold ankle chain had little jingle bells on it, which would make sounds every time I took a step down the stairs, and the jingle sound would sometimes wake up the boys from their dreams. I would open up all the shutters in the house, watching the sun rise. The blue moon Wisteria Vine would be hanging over the windows and I could touch the flowers with my hands, and the softness of the flower felt soothing to me as I picked a few to put in a vase on the breakfast table which was standing towards the back of the house. I would lift my baby Charlie up from his crib and walk over to the window for him to touch the vine with his tiny soft fingers. We would all sit down at the dining table, which had old ceramic vintage Italian tiles on the surface and beautiful big wicker armchairs that I had painted turquoise set around the table. The chairs had big soft white linen fabric cushion covers with a pattern of pale pink wild roses on them. I would stroke my oldest son Oliver's hair as he sat next to me eating a soft-boiled egg and toast and fresh orange juice, and I would have a vegetable smoothie while I was breastfeeding my baby Charlie lying on my lap on top of a cushion, his little feet covered in a pair of white, hand-knitted baby booties, hanging over the cushion.

Me and Phil would be talking about walking down to the marketplace by Antibes harbour, which had the most amazing looking sail boats rocking against each other, and the sound of the boats would often make my baby Charlie doze off in the pram.

We would sit at the marketplace watching people walking by, smelling the gorgeous scent of lavender bouquets wrapped in purple gift sheets tied with hand-dyed straw strings in all rainbow colours.

We had friends living in the same street as us, and we often hung out around each other's houses. I met Lawrence and Jaleh who lived opposite us and realised that I used to go to Lawrence's hair salon, Crimpers, back in London years before moving to France. I didn't know Lawrence then, as I had my hair cut by one of his assistants, but I do remember seeing him in the salon; when I looked at his face, I recognised him from the past. The synchronicity still amazes me, not knowing then that we would live next door to each other one day in France, fifteen years later.

We lived in Antibes for five years before moving back to England again. In that period, I now had two boys and a dog, and the traumas with Phil were starting to grow, not knowing that he had a mistress in Italy.

Divorce Papers

Moving back to England was a big change of life and the tension between me and Phil became worse for years to come, as I sadly didn't find out he had a mistress behind my back for many years.

It's a part of my life that seems to be a blur of confusion and sadness. Our marriage was over many years before we went our own ways and the blessing of the divorce papers landing unexpectedly on my doorstep on a warm day in August 2011. I felt very sad that thirty-two years of marriage was now over. Somehow over time I saw light at the end of the tunnel, and it gave me the strength to find my own identity by changing my life around. It opened up many doors for me and the boys, and calmness and love for each other came bouncing back into our lives.

I had the '*om*' sign tattooed on the inside of my left arm, close to my wrist area, exactly one month to the day after I received the divorce papers. . .

Om is a spiritual symbol which refers to Atman (soul, self within). It also signifies the essence of the ultimate reality, consciousness of Atman.

The Big House

I loved the little cottage I had bought two roads from where I had lived before in a much bigger house, and which I had made into a beautiful home. Friends walking into the big house always told me it was like walking into a house situated on a sandy beach. I had all the walls through the house painted the colour of magnolia. And our furniture was in shades of yellow, bluebell colours and dusty greens.

The house was full of plants from jasmines, roses, big ferns hanging from the ceiling, and I always had a big bouquet of lily flowers on the cast iron dining table which had six wicker wingback lounge chairs around it, covered in lemon colour silk cushions, which blended in so beautifully with the ferns hanging in baskets over the dining table. I loved the dining room floor which was covered in vintage ceramic mosaic Italian tiles, and the ceiling had beautiful natural round skylights.

The dining room had big double doors out to the garden which was full of trees and flowers covering the wooden fences all around the garden. There was a big willow tree in the middle of the garden where I had a tree-hugger bench put around it, and I used to sit there with the boys, looking up at the midnight sky when there was a full moon. It was so bright as it shone on their beautiful faces, and I could see the reflection of the moon in their eyes, and I would wrap them in my quilt all together and it felt wonderful to just sit there in silence. These were the moments with the boys I will always treasure as gold.

I had an artist who painted red roses on the bedroom chest of drawers, and I had bought a pale-yellow silk bedspread to cover the big Danish Dux bed which has followed my journey around the world. I used to lay myself on the bed late at night, cover myself up in big silk cushions with hand-sewn bluebells on them, crying my eyes out over why Phil had been unfaithful to me for so many years. I didn't know, until I got a phone call from his now wife, telling me that Phil wanted a divorce as she was getting married to him as soon as the divorce went through.

I was in shock as I had no idea who she was, and Phil was in total denial when I asked him who she was. It took months before he admitted to me that he had known her for years, and was getting very confused with his own lies. I was devastated of knowing the truth at last!

CHAPTER 52

Snugli

I moved to my little cottage after I was forced to leave my big house with my two boys, a house I had been so passionate about and loved so dearly.

So many beautiful memories of my two boys went through my mind as I locked the front door for the last time, not looking back but blowing the house goodbye kisses. As I stood there bewildered and wondering what the future would bring, I fell into dreaming of the past, seeing my youngest boy Charlie growing up in the house from nursery school to an adult. Being born in France and spending a lot of time by the sea when he was a baby, I would put him in a wraparound sling which was made of this beautiful African aquamarine fabric which felt soft against his newborn skin. In the sixties, a woman called Ann Moore developed a baby carrier she called 'Snugli'. I loved that word, and I would say to my baby Charlie, 'Let's put you in Snugli.' And he knew we would be walking down to the beach and sitting in the sand early in the evening when there were no people around, and we would have the whole coastline to ourselves. I would give him a bottle of apple juice that I had packed in my old musty-coloured rucksack, along with a small bottle of red wine and multi-coloured olives bought in the marketplace. I had brought one of my Danish royal Holmegaard wine glasses with me too. I let my baby have a little taste of the wine on my finger, which he liked. I would drape myself and my baby into my lavender-coloured linen blanket and we would watch the sun go down, seeing the sky turning into this beautiful pale tint of orange, while I was massaging his tiny soft feet which had unfolded from their wrinkles into smooth baby skin and had taken a few steps holding on to my hands. While I was massaging his tiny feet lying in my lap, I would sing a lullaby: 'Hush little baby, don't say a word, Papa's gonna buy you a mockingbird.' He would fall into a dream world, and I would put him back in 'Snugli' and walk home under the moonlight to our house not far from the beach. I would lay myself down on our bed with my baby next to me, giving him breast milk while I was looking at his small round face with red cheeks from the evening sun. I would cover us both in the lavender linen blanket which smelled of the seashore. A few grains of sand were still in between his tiny toes, and I would wipe them away with the edge of my sleeveless long lime-green dress, and I would watch the fireflies glowing in the night making a circle around me and my baby, protecting us in the moonlight.

Charlie Chaplin

I was still standing at the front door visualising Charlie being three years old and taking him to the Montessori nursery school, which was developed by Italian physician, Maria Montessori, in the early nineties. Based on her observations, she believed that children who are at liberty to choose and act freely within an environment prepared according to her model would act spontaneously for optimal development. I was thinking of a moment in time when I picked Charlie up from nursery. I was looking at his lovely face when he was standing there in the locker room smiling at me from ear to ear happy to see me as he wanted to show me how he could put his blue woollen winter coat on himself. He spread the coat out on the floor where he put the sleeves out to the sides, and he placed himself down on the coat. He would slide his arms into the sleeves and get up again and he would be wearing his coat perfectly, and I would do the buttons up and tell him, 'What a magical way of putting your coat on!' We hugged and he would put his red leather boots on. Putting the left boot on his right foot, and the right boot on his left foot, we would walk out to the schoolyard hand in hand, and I would kiss his little red cheeks, which were burning from the big effort of putting his clothes on himself. I let him walk in front of me and I couldn't help giggling as he was walking like Charlie Chaplin and all he needed was a bamboo cane and a bowler hat.

These moments of joy were so precious to me with all the memories of Oliver too, both growing up together in that house. And here we were, hugging all the rooms as we said our goodbyes to the house, and hoping the new owners would love the house as much as we did. By then Phil had left the country to live with his mistress in Italy. They married not long after our divorce.

CHAPTER 53

The Little Cottage

Standing in my little cottage hallway opening up the letter (which was supposed to go to my lawyer's office) was a day I will never forget.

I sat myself on my dusty old green couch, feeling my warm tears running down my face. I wrapped myself into the patchwork throw my grandmother had given me which always soothed me when I felt some kind of pain, and I read the line saying, 'It is hereby certified that the said decree was on the 22nd of August 2011, made final and absolute and the marriage is thereby dissolved.'

I had to tell the boys the divorce was final, and that night I was lying on my youngest son Charlie's bed with him, hugging him tight, trying to comfort him as he wouldn't stop crying. By then his big brother, Oliver, had moved to an apartment, as I only had two bedrooms in my little cottage.

Through the years to come there were a lot of traumas with the boys not having their dad around any more, which was hard on me. I tried to be both parents for many years, and their dad would come to visit us, but there were always too many tears shed when he was around. I told him not to come into the house any more, and pick up Charlie by the front door, as his mistress would also make sure that he never entered the cottage.

The little cottage became a healing place to live over the next three years. I made the cottage into a sanctuary with our belongings from the big house and I had chimes hanging everywhere, so when the wind was blowing through the house, it sounded like a symphony orchestra playing a wonderful melody. . .

The small back garden had a little wooden shed I painted bluebell colour, and I filled up the ground with wildflowers, roses and lavender. I planted a small willow tree and put snow-drops and crocuses underneath the tree, and I bought an old vintage ornately-detailed cement bird bath where I had birds taking their morning baths every morning while I was sitting with my morning coffee in a cup my boys had given me, with 'Love you Mum' on it. I would make toast with strawberry jam, enjoying watching the birds having their morning showers, spreading their wings to get water underneath them.

I felt blessed that I had moved forward, and the boys seemed more contented in life. I joined a yoga class in my neighbour-hood which helped me believe in myself and I was worthy of loving myself and being respected for who I am as a woman.

CHAPTER 54

Blossoming Like a Rose

I would wake up in the morning putting my tracksuit and Ugg boots on, and put my hair up in a ponytail with a scarf my grandmother used to wear around her head. Later in life, I made the scarf into a cushion cover, and wrapped it around Charlie's old baby pillow. I have put it against the back of an old antique wicker chair I have in my bathroom and I always think of my dear grandmother wearing her scarf on a windy day. . . I used to drop Charlie off at the school gate and kiss his little round face, telling him, 'I love you and I will see you again this afternoon.' I would walk to yoga class and sit myself on the yoga mat which became a lifeline for many years to come. I started to feel alive again and my whole being blossomed like a rose opening its petals, while the sun rays caressed my skin, feeling and looking youthful again. I'm thankful for my lovely yoga teacher Rachel who helped me to see the light at the other end of the dark tunnel I went through for a long time.

I loved the classes of not more than ten people; we would be like a little family for an hour, and at the end of the session we would lie down and meditate next to each other. Often, we would fall asleep and the sounds of some of us snoring was a soothing sound to me of feeling peaceful, and perhaps spiritually we were one in those moments in time.

We would wake up and say our goodbyes until we met again the following week. We never really talked to each other as it didn't matter who we were or where we came from in our lives. I loved that silence between us and yet we knew each other in that room. It was an old church hall, and I loved when the teacher Rachel would open the windows and we could hear the birds singing in the trees and smell the flowers blowing their fragrance through the windows. I'm wondering where these beautiful people are today.

Yoga and the counselling with Jasmine saved my sanity; I got to know who I was as I slowly came back to living a life that gave me back the confidence of the forgotten creativity I had always had in me, but was taken away from me over the years in the dysfunctional marriage me and Phil had lived for far too many years. I realised that getting the divorce papers on my doorstep was a blessing; it meant moving on and at last being who I was supposed to be, and my relationship with the boys became peaceful. The musical chimes in the little cottage house took me back to when I was a child; I loved watching the old black-and-white Hollywood movies with the wooden cabins in the mountains, surrounded by the beautiful pine trees with the fireplaces lit and people sitting outside on their porch on a swing or rocking chairs, playing music on their banjos or violins and talking about life while the chimes swung in the warm breeze around the fire and played their own tunes. . .

How amazing that three years later I would be travelling to North Carolina, sitting on a swing on a porch listening to my friend playing on his mouth harmonica and taking trips on a Harley Davidson motorbike.

CHAPTER 55

More Healing

Before my journey took me to North Carolina, I moved to Muswell Hill in north London in 2014, once my two boys were established in their own worlds in the city where we had lived together in the little cottage.

I moved to Muswell Hill because I wanted to revisit the time I had spent there with Phil and our boys. Funny that Phil was born in a house in Denmark Street, as were his uncles Dave and Ray Davies. I also wanted to move out of my comfort zone town where I had lived for years with Phil and the boys.

It was a healing process for me to live in that area, walking the streets and the parks where we were once a family. We used to take Oliver to the parks when he was a little boy. I can still see him in Golders Hill Park on a skateboard his dad had bought him in Los Angeles. He would sit holding onto the middle of it and then glide down the hill until I couldn't see him any more, only the silhouette of his sweet little body holding on tight. His long black hair would be blowing away from his face and his multi-coloured scarf around his neck seemed to blend in with the green trees passing him by.

I can see him standing on the top of the hill, holding onto his kite with his glowing cheeks from the wind blowing into his face. He was wearing his warm blue woolly coat and red knitted hat and black lace-up boots. He would be running down the hill with the kite and letting it go before he ran into my arms feeling warm and safe. So many beautiful moments in time in Golders Hill Park. . .

It helped me to reminisce about the past living in Muswell Hill, to move forward but keep the past in a precious little magic box - little things like the boys' first pairs of shoes, their milk teeth I have put in the magic box, love letters from Phil, photos of us all. The magic box will always be with me on my journey as I never want to forget those moments in time.

Sacred Nest

I felt amazing being me again in my sacred nest, even though I missed the boys terribly. Living an hour away from me, they would come and visit me often. It was a one-bedroom maisonette with a beautiful back garden. I have memories of sitting on one of my turquoise-painted wicker chairs filled with big flowery cushions in my new sanctuary garden, bare-foot in my soft pale blue cotton pyjamas and wrapped in my grandmother's quilt. I felt warm as I tugged my legs up to my chest with a cup of hot herbal tea with a slice of lemon, and a bowl of porridge with a pinch of cinnamon on top. I was admiring my creativity, looking at my big blue pots around the wooden deck, filled with wild pale pink roses I had dug up from my last garden. I wanted to have something with me which made me think of the little cottage where me and the boys had started a new life, just the three of us. The fragrance of the roses felt very uplifting as a new chapter of my journey started to unfold itself, living on my own and just enjoying the peace I was surrounded by.

I had made a meditation corner at the back of the garden, with chimes hanging from the trees and my big spiritual Buddha statue surrounded by candles. I had put my selection of crystal stones which had cleansing and clarity healing properties in front of my Buddha. I would hold my stones in my hands when I was sitting on my serenity meditation chair and just breathe deeply in and out and smell the fragrance of the wild roses when there was a little breeze in the air. I would always put a rose in my long hair hanging over my shoulders when I was meditating. It really was the beginning of my healing, putting all the traumatising years behind me.

My sacred nest became a peaceful place surrounded by things I loved. I had a dark red velvet fabric put on the old couch standing in my living room, with thousands of multi-coloured silk cushions laid out on it. A big vintage armchair covered in pale pink cotton fabric. Indian rugs on the wooden floors, crystal chandeliers and candles everywhere. All the old paintings from my past two houses were now hanging on the walls, telling a lot of the history of my past life of being a family for many, many years. I would always be thinking about the loving and happy times we had when I fell into my dreams looking at them.

My bedroom had a fireplace which had beautiful old vintage pale green ceramic tiles around it, and I had hung my big vintage cream-colour wooden-framed mirror up above the fireplace. My dear artist friend hand-painted ivy branches all around the frame on it, and I felt I was in the forest among trees of life when I looked at myself in the mirror, amazed how the colour of my skin had started to glow.

I filled up my little bathroom with colourful towels and chimes hanging from the ceiling, and crystals lying in a little bowl my friend in Barbados had made for me out of coconuts. I had a skylight in the bathroom which I opened up when I had showers and if there was a breeze of wind, they would whistle a melody for me.

I spent two years out of my life in this sacred nest I had made for myself and I became healthier and happier through that year, ready to travel the world again.

CHAPTER 56

North Carolina

I woke up one morning on a warm late summer day in 2014, and the sound of the birds singing in the trees as my bedroom window was open in my sacred nest made my day start in a calming way.

I put on my old vintage turquoise cotton tracksuit trousers I had bought back in Barbados in the eighties, and a white zipper tracksuit top and put on the old lemon green suede trainers bought in Los Angeles, which had seen better days. They had faded over the years and looked more of a musty grey now. I tied my hair back and put my grandmother's scarf around my head and made a big bow on top of my head. I thought I would jog to the café and sit with my cappuccino, and sunbathe my face in the beautiful courtyard at the back of the café. There were honeysuckles hanging over the fences and big couches to sit on, and they always had fresh flowers on the tables which smelled divine in beautiful old vintage glass vases. The smell of the honeysuckle was overwhelming and filled the air with so many uplifting thoughts of what was next for me to explore.

I had friends in North Carolina who had invited me to come over to the US and stay with them. I had been thinking about it for a while and that morning, sitting at the café, I thought why not! I was on a flight two days later going to North Carolina, and a new adventure was ahead of me.

Fayetteville

I arrived at Raleigh Durham Airport after a long flight and my friend came to pick me up in his very old blue Ford pick-up truck. We arrived at the house two hours later in the town of Fayetteville and his dog Smiley welcomed me into the house licking me all over. Smiley became my best friend on this trip. I loved the view from the front of the house over the cotton and tobacco fields which apparently cover 900,000 acres of North Carolina to this day.

It was a landscape I had never seen before, and it took my breath away. There was a very dark red barn at the back of the garden, which was the first time I had seen a barn and I loved it, as it took me back again to my childhood, watching the old American movies from the Midwest. There was a porch at the front of the house with a white painted swing on it where I would often sit with Smiley at sunrise with my morning coffee and toast with lots of butter on it and a sprinkle of cinnamon, which seems to be a very American breakfast. I would be swinging backwards and forwards on the swing in my pale blue loose linen overalls and a tight white sleeveless T-shirt. I had bare feet and a multi-coloured beaded ankle chain bracelet on each ankle which I had bought on my travels to Barbados. My outback western straw cowboy hat fitted my head fine and I felt so alive sitting there on the swing with Smiley by my feet, trying to lick them every time I went forward on the swing, hoping I would share my toast with her too, looking at me with her big brown eyes.

It was like time was standing still. You would see a car in the distance passing by the house maybe every hour, and I started to feel very at ease with myself, as there was no one telling me what to do or where to go or how to be. Things just happened when they did. My friend had an even older white and pale blue Ford grandpa truck from 1965 which he was repairing. We would take a drive up his long path by the house on a rainy day, and the window wipers made this old shrieking sound which reminded me of my favourite movie *The Bridges of Madison County* which I have watched a million times. The moment in the movie where Meryl Streep and her husband are waiting for the red traffic lights to change to green on a rainy day. She doesn't know if she wants to get out of the car leaving her husband for her lover, Clint Eastwood, who is parked on the other side of the road; she's holding around the car door handle very tight, wanting to open the door, but decides to stay in the car and the traffic lights turn green, and she looks in the back mirror seeing Clint Eastwood's face though the car window fading away as they drive off. She will never see her lover again. I loved that moment in the movie.

The time in North Carolina was a great healer for me, just 'being', never knowing what we were doing from day to day. One day my friend Monte asked me if I felt up to going on a trip further north to visit his friends Ernie and Beth on his Harley motorbike. I felt a little afraid of riding on a Harley, as I had never been on a motorbike before. I bought a Harley Davidson leather jacket and boots covering my legs up to the knees. The next day came around and we took off on the Harley. I felt the adrenalin rising in my body. I thought to myself: *I must be crazy but, what the hell, why not!*

The experience of taking off on the bike was mind-blowing. I felt I had wings and I was flying through the air. The scenery around us was stunningly beautiful, passing the tobacco fields and beautiful farms with wild horses grazing on the grass. We would be riding around sharp bends, more or less sitting sideways, our knees nearly touching the ground. We would stop in typical American diners serving fast food, where we ordered a pile of pancakes with syrup and over-easy eggs and hash browns, it would keep us going through the long rides.

Kentucky

We would also take a drive in the old blue Ford pick-up truck to Kentucky to visit family. I loved the old covered bridges we would be crossing, which are still standing from being built in the 18th century. I remember the sound of the truck's creaking wheels when we crossed the bridges, and the river flowing underneath was soothing to me. We would be jumping up and down in the old leather seats, and I would have my arm hanging out of the window, feeling the warm breeze against my skin and reaching out for the rail bars which were covered in ivy.

When we arrived at the house of Monte's sister Marlene and her husband Billy who lived in Louisville, I felt like I had walked into a house from the fifties. I walked into the kitchen, where there was a Coca-Cola dinette set with four classic Coke chairs with chrome-plated frames. The table had steel chrome-plated legs and the most beautiful retro 1950s tablecloth with tropical leaves on it. The 1950s Chambers stove was placed underneath a window that had vintage floral print cotton curtains pulled to the sides with big, twisted strings tied into bows.

I loved that kitchen and I fell into my dreams of being in an old 1950s movie. I would be wearing a retro rockabilly princess Cosplay floral halter-neck dress and a pair of flat leather loafers, sitting myself down on one of the Coca-Cola chairs and listening to Johnny Cash singing 'Walk the Line' while I drank a Coca-Cola.

I went into the bedroom and, looking out of the big old windows and right across the road, I saw an old Kentucky steam locomotive passing the house. It would pass the house many times through the day, and at night I fell asleep listening to the old steam train carriages trundling along on the rails. At the end of the empty street, there was a crossing with a traffic light hanging on a string, swaying from side to side in the warm breeze and the lights would change from red to amber, from amber to green every five minutes, even though there were no cars crossing.

The Uptown Café

There was one café called 'The Uptown Café' where I hung out in the mornings wearing my old 1950s Washington blue overall jeans and a white cotton T-shirt and the old suede cowboy boots and my forever old felt hat with a rose from the garden around the brim. I would have a chat with the owners of the café who were a very eccentric couple. They spoke in a very Southern accent, and it was difficult for me to understand what they were saying. The wife had hardly any teeth in her mouth, and she smoked a pipe. She had long dark brown, curly, braided hair that hung over her breasts down to her waist and her clothes fascinated me as, again, they seemed to have been taken out of a movie. She had men's oversize vintage denim jeans on, held up with a beautiful western turquoise buckle belt and a 1950's polka dot rockabilly cotton shirt, and she was walking around in bare feet. I asked her name, while I sat myself down on one of their retro pinewood tables. She told me her name was Jocelyn and it means 'cheerful'. I loved her name and I told her my name was Jette. She pronounced my name perfectly as the Americans do, as they never pronounce their T's! She said, 'Nice to meet you, Yedde.'

We had a long chat about how she ended up living in Kentucky as she came from Texas. She introduced me to her husband who was from Kentucky. He had a long beard and big brown eyes and grey long hair put up in a ponytail. He smiled at me with his surprisingly white teeth and shook my hand with his big hard-working hands which had seen a lot of labour over the years. He told me his name was Joe. He also walked around barefoot and told me he played in a band at night in the only bar in town. I said to him I would love to see him play that night, and I said my goodbyes.

The Florist Lady

I walked the last bit of the street and passed by the florist shop where there was a ginger cat with a black nose lying in the window, sunbathing in the middle of all the flower arrangements as the late afternoon sun was shining through the window on its body. The florist lady sat on a cast iron bench outside the front of the shop, making a beautiful bouquet of lilies and white wild roses, binding them together. She told me it was a wedding bouquet for her niece getting married that afternoon. I sat next to her on the cast iron bench for a while, talking to her about life, and she told me she had visited London in the seventies in a town called Southgate. I couldn't believe what I heard as that is the town I was living in when I was working as an au pair back then. Another synchronicity of perhaps having crossed each other's paths on the other side of the world.

She was a lovely woman with wavy blonde curly hair, which was all tied up on top of her head with a retro butterfly hair comb that was decorated in silver and turquoise stones. Her beautiful vintage high-waisted long musty yellow dress was clinging to her very narrow waist and her tiny ankles looked so petite in her little flat white loafers. I told her I was going down to the bar tonight to listen to Joe and his band playing on their banjos and fiddles, and she told me she would come down. I walked back to Monte's sister Marlene's house, and felt I had been experiencing another adventure of meeting lovely people in this quirky little town.

We all went down to the bar that night and had beers and a dance on the old wooden floor which was made of old railway track wooden sleepers. It made a wonderfully distinctive clunk from people's cowboy boots as the heels hit the floor sooner than the foot. The old steam train on the railway track would pass the bar, trundling along and blowing its horn, mixed with the sounds of Joe's band playing their music. What a night to remember.

The time passed very quickly, just hanging out with friends in North Carolina, and it was a very healing time for me to move forward, travelling the roads for the next couple of years. I lived in England in my safe sacred nest for a few months and then I would travel back to North Carolina for a couple of months, and in those years, I started to feel better and better within myself, and I really started to blossom.

I'm thankful for the time I spent in North Carolina with dear friends, and I hope to see them again some day.

As my journey continued, I travelled to Colorado for my dear friend Teresa's daughter's wedding in 2016 and I fell in love with Niwot town. Amazingly Colorado became my home a couple of years later.

CHAPTER 57

Bubble of Darkness

Living in Niwot in 2016 in my little rented apartment in Kathy's house on and off through time over the next three years, was such a lovely healing nest filled with Buddhas, chimes, big bohemian cushions, feathers and couches, native Indian rugs on floor and walls, and some of my paintings shipped over from England were now hanging on the walls. I was living in a bubble of tranquillity, serenity and calmness, and meditated every morning before the sunrise. I took long walks in the mountains where I learned to listen to the sound of trees, birds singing, and eagles flying high above my head. The blue skies with mind-blowing clouds in all shapes and forms, inspired me to take up photography which I have enjoyed ever since I moved to Colorado. So many years of the past I had lived in a bubble of darkness.

The Beach Hut Painting

To continue my healing, I travelled to Barbados on my own in 2017. I rented the house I had been staying at many times before. It is a sanctuary of blissfulness close to Gibbs Beach and, on my arrival at Barbados Airport late at night, I got into a taxi, which took me through all the familiar windy roads where the sugar cane and banana plantations grew high above us, and it felt like another adventure was ahead of me.

I arrived at the house late at night and I said hello to Leah, my dear friend of many years. She said, 'Welcome back,' and we hugged. I went into the familiar rooms, and it felt good to be back in my second home. I unpacked my suitcase and opened the white painted shutters, and the warm breeze of air would softly touch my face as I wrapped myself in my pale pink linen kimono. I braided my hair and put it up in a bun on top of my head as it was a warm tropical night. I sat myself under the palm trees, listening to the sound of the big palm leaves swaying from side to side in the warm breeze and watching the fireflies twinkling like little stars. I picked up a coconut which had fallen from the tree above me; I would have the delicious coconut milk for breakfast the next morning. It was a full moon night, and I was dozing off under the stars, listening to the musical entertainment of whistling frogs as the bats began their crazy nocturnal airborne aerobics.

*

It was a typical day in Barbados when I woke up in my bed after a long sleep. Deborah, my dear friend who worked at the house, had put my blue flowery flannel sheet on my bed the night before which I had left there the last time I was at the house, and she had put it on a shelf in the washroom for my return, which was so kind of her. I was happy to see and feel it on the bed the night before. It was very soothing to me, as my grandmother had given it to me long time ago, and I always packed it in my suitcase through my travels. It was nice to have my grandmother with me in my dreams at night. . .

My little painting of 'the beach hut' which my lovely friend, Annette, had painted also came with me on my travels. I hung it up over my bed in my bedroom (and I have it in my studio today, hanging above my typewriter where all the magic writing happens). My old musty green felt hat would be hanging next to the painting, and I felt I had all the loving things around me, and a photo of my boys next to my bed, so I could say good morning to them on my early rising and goodnight at sunset. I opened the shutters and my friendly little bird I called Winston would be sitting on top of the kitchen shutters, waiting for me to prepare my cereals with added sliced bananas that I had picked from the trees, and strawberries I knew Winston liked to share with me. He sat on the edge of my breakfast bowl happily eating the strawberries, and we became close friends through my time in the house.

I took the bus into Holetown after breakfast. I said my good-byes to Winston and walked five minutes down to the bus stop wearing my retro country button-down floral dress and an old pair of flat black canvas shoes, and I let my long hair hang over my shoulders. I felt sweat dripping down at the back of my neck as it was a very hot morning, and I wiped my neck with the silk handkerchief with the hand-embroidered red roses on it that my grandmother had sewn on her sewing machine. I had dabbed a little vintage Jasmine Breeze cologne on it, as it reminded me of my grandmother's scent when we hugged.

The bus stop was just opposite a house called Mischief. While I was waiting for the bus, I saw my four-year-old son Oliver on the balcony of the Mischief house where Phil and I had stayed in 1988. Memories came flowing back of Oliver running to me in his little vibrant green sandals and wearing his Oshkosh blue denim overalls over his bare chest. He was so tanned from being on the beach all day and he put his little arms around my neck, and we hugged and the cool breeze from the sea felt cooling on our bodies. . .

As I stood there dreaming, waiting for the bus, I realised that I was surrounded by palm trees with their massive green leaves hanging over the road and the bus driver wouldn't be able to see me. I stepped out on the road and put my arm out so he could see me waving at him.

Delicious Chicken

I got on the bus and gave the bus driver $2 for the ride, and he smiled from ear to ear with his white teeth shining like diamonds. He had big chunky gold necklaces around his neck, and his girlfriend with rollers in her hair sat next to him in the front window, eating a hamburger. I sat myself down on the old lilac leather seats, listening to reggae music on full volume as we rolled down the bumpy winding roads; mothers with their babies were breast feeding and holding them up over their shoulders to get them to burp.

A guy with a full head of dreadlocks and the most beautiful smile sat next to me, and he asked, 'Do you want to share my spicy chicken with me?'

'Yes, that would be lovely and thank you,' I said, 'this is a very tasty and delicious chicken.' He smiled at me as I got off at my bus stop, and I said, 'Nice meeting you and maybe I will see you on the bus tomorrow.'

He said, 'I hope so.' I never asked what his name was but, it really didn't matter as to me he was just a nice guy sharing his chicken with me. . .

Methodist Church

I walked across the street to Holetown Methodist Church. I sat myself down on one of the beautiful solid oak pews and looked up at the enchanting blue stained-glass church windows and just sat in silence as the cool breeze from outside was flowing through the church; it felt good feeling cooler after the warm bus ride. I lit a candle whose shadows flickered on the wall, looking like a ballerina dancing in her long-sleeved white handkerchief dress.

A little girl came into the church. She had a beautiful face and her very thick braided black hair was split in two ponytails which had very vibrant bright yellow ribbons wrapped around each ponytail. She sat herself down next to me and she was wearing a floral sequined black princess dress with a yellow rose sewn into the waistline. She put her hand in mine and looked at me with her big brown eyes, and we just sat there for a while and we never spoke, and then she stood up and walked out of the church and I never saw her again. Perhaps she was trying to tell me something; I will never know.

I walked over to the café and had my delicious cappuccino which always came with a home-cooked almond biscuit, straight out of the oven. I watched people walking by in their beautiful colourful Caribbean clothing. I was mesmerised by the women's stunningly beautiful hairstyles as if they were pieces of art. I felt like sitting there all day and just daydreaming, but I got back on the bus heading for the beach.

Green Monkeys

I got off the bus and walked up the hill to my house among the trees with the Barbadians green monkeys climbing above me, jumping from one tree to the other, the little baby monkeys clinging firmly to their mother's stomach rooting for her nipples in mid-air before the mother would reach the next tree. The monkeys sometimes walked by my house in the afternoon and sat in the deckchairs by the pool when I opened up the shutters again. They were drinking the milk from the coconuts which had fallen to the ground overnight while I sat close by, watching them and listening to their very high-pitched vocal language, wondering what they were talking about.

I walked into my house and put a bouquet of Barbados wildflowers in a vase, mostly Bougainvillea, Desert Rose and Hibiscus that I'd picked along the roadside from my walk back to the house after getting off the bus. I put the flowers on the dining table, and at night I put the flowers outside on the terrace on my bamboo table and I felt enchanted by how they shone beautifully in the moonlight.

Barefoot In the Sand

I packed my fifties vintage white woven wicker bag with bottles of water, sun cream and little snacks, and wrapped a yellow sweet pea wildflower around the handle which smelled divine while I was walking down to the beach. I had put my faded violet-pink towel over my shoulders and my flowery cherry-blossom colour long strappy dress was blowing up around my waist from the breeze of wind as I got closer to Gibbs Beach. The sea air felt so good around my legs, and I took off my old canvas lace-up boots, feeling the warm white sand underneath my feet like a gentle foot massage.

After a swim in the beautiful turquoise silk water, I sat in the warm sand wrapped in my towel, looking along the very edge of the sea front and I had a vision of going back in time to 1988, watching my little boy Oliver running barefoot in the warm sand. I could still hear him calling me with his sweet voice to come and build sandcastles with him. We made a beautiful sandcastle with holes looking like windows and put Barbadian white lilies in them. We walked on the sand to the beach bar holding his soft little hand in mine. He had a little bead bracelet around his wrist, which I played with as we walked along, counting the beads with him. We sat on the old wooden floorboards on benches that were falling apart and looked out to the turquoise sea, watching the boats sailing by.

He fell asleep in my lap, and I wrapped him in my towel and walked back to our house, gently putting him down on his bed while the sound of the waves made me sleepy too and we cuddled up and slept until sunrise. . .

Ole on the Beach

Coming out of my dreams of Oliver and me on the beach, I saw an old man with his dog walking down the path to the beach. I had seen him every day walking down the hill past my house and wondered where he was going. My local friend was passing me by on the beach and I asked him if he knew the old man. He said he did, his name was Ole and he was Danish. 'You should go and say hello to him,' he told me, and I did. We started to talk in Danish when I told him I was Danish too.

From that day, we became dear friends for many years, and I have visited his beautiful gardens many times over the years.

When I visited Ole's gardens, I was overwhelmed by all the beauty he had made out of a big piece of land he had bought forty-five years before.

That afternoon, after my swim and meeting Ole on the beach, we walked up to his house just up the hill from where I was staying. We sat on his terrace in his gardens overlooking the panorama of beauty as if it had been taken out of the movie *Out of Africa*, sipping ice cold pineapple juice he grew in his gardens. I looked at Ole in his old, faded overalls and his worn-out brown Danish clogs, wearing his old forest-green felt hat and his glasses perched on the tip of his perfectly straight nose, wondering how he kept his glasses in place. He told me he had made this beautiful garden of Eden a true paradise sanctuary from little seeds he had brought home in his pockets on his world travels.

We walked around his garden and he told me stories of each little seed he had planted on his land and which countries he had brought the seeds back from to Barbados. His orchid sanctuary filled the air with the aroma they produce to attract pollinators like bees, butterflies and hummingbirds.

I picked avocados, lemons, tomatoes, cucumbers and aubergines among other vegetables he grew, and put them into an old native American picnic basket Ole gave me, with two handles on it and a lid on both sides. It had beautiful, coiled fibre native art designs woven on it, and I loved the smell of the basket that evening after I emptied it out of all the wonderful treasures I had been given by Ole. I made a vegetable stew and so enjoyed eating it, and I can still taste all the flavours in my mouth to this day.

After long magical days in Barbados from sunrise to sunset, always ending the days sitting under the palm trees looking at the stars, was my daily routines of blissfulness.

Sadly, Ole passed away in 2019. He was flown home to Denmark, and he is now shining like a twinkling star in the sky and his spirit will still be in his garden of Eden, shining bright forever.

When I go back to Barbados, I will see him in spirit on the beach, walking into the turquoise sea with his dog and swimming together, still wearing his old forest green felt hat and his head just above water. He will be swimming sideways, and we will meet in the sea, our toes touching the sand, getting the last bit of evening light on our bodies, talking about life and what we have both seen in many beautiful places on this earth.

*

Life works in mysterious ways as I travelled to Barbados with my husband James in 2018, and we visited Ole, and I had a feeling that it would be the last time I hugged him as he had been ill for a very long time. . .

CHAPTER 58

Brown Eyes

I met James back in Niwot where I lived at the time in 2018, at the restaurant where we met for the first time, and I have called Twin Peaks all through my memoir. The real name of the restaurant was Treppeda's, where James knew the owner well, and I'm sure we had been in the restaurant many times in the past at the same time but never looked into each other's eyes before the day my dear friend, Nancy, introduced us to each other. From then on, we never stopped talking.

It was like life stood still and people's voices around us became a distant humming that didn't make sense to me. We only had eyes for each other. I noticed his beautiful brown eyes looking at me through his little round glasses, and his beautiful hands. He had a white cotton shirt on which clung to his chest, and worn-out pale blue jeans and cream leather boots with a zip on the side. We started to talk about our lives as we had both been married before. I told him that I had been coming to Colorado ever since the late seventies and that Teresa, who I met at Caribou Ranch, had been my dear friend ever since I lived in England, and we always wrote to each other and talked on the phone through the years of us both getting married and having children. I will never forget the expression on James's face when he said, 'You don't mean Teresa Taylor?'

I said, 'Yes, do you know her?' He told me that he lived right across the street from her and had lived there for thirty years with his late wife.

I felt I was dreaming, as we must have crossed each other's paths many times over the years, living our lives in different countries in different worlds. I saw myself and Oliver, who was five years old at the time, visiting Teresa's house and James sitting in his front garden under his willow tree looking at me through his little round glasses, wondering who I was. We could not have imagined then the magic of the synchronicity of me sitting underneath the same willow tree with him thirty years later.

I still lived in Niwot, feeling very much intrigued by this lovely man who had entered my life unexpectedly with the charm and intelligence of a well-read man, having interesting conversations with each other over many romantic dinners. Love for each other grew fast through the time we spent together over the next six months.

In July the same year that I met James, he invited me on a trip to Greece. We travelled around the islands, a country we hadn't been to before. We both fell in love with Greece and with each other and hoped to go back to visit Greece again someday.

At the end of our beautiful trip in Greece we had to say our goodbyes, as I was flying to England for my oldest son's wedding and James flew back to the US.

Wedding in the Barn

I landed at Heathrow Airport on the 25th of July so excited about my oldest son's wedding two days later. My dear friend

Annie came to pick me up at the airport as I was staying at her house.

The night before the wedding, I was dreaming of Oliver being a little boy taking his first footsteps when he was one year old. I remember I was standing in the kitchen in our first house, and I looked around and Oliver walked towards me in his little blue and white striped Oshkosh overalls. The legs were rolled up twice as they were too long, and he wore his little red leather Danish slippers which had ankle straps with a little white pearl button. He walked very fast on his cute little legs and just made it as he fell into my arms. We hugged and I wrapped him inside my long beaded dusty cream cardigan he always loved to hide in, and felt the comfort of feeling warm against my body heat. I put his long hair behind his ears so I could see his lovely face smiling at me, and I told him how proud I was of him taking his first ten footsteps.

When I woke up on the morning of the wedding day, I was overwhelmed with emotions. I could see Oliver holding onto his little friend Pink Panther before bedtime in his cute snug Snoopy pajamas which had cotton buttons on the back, and he would put Pink Panther into his vintage wooden bed which had wooden wheels on it so I could wheel it into our bedroom at night if he wasn't happy sleeping in his own room. He would cover Pink Panther up in his cotton quilt which was handmade in India. It had hand-carved wooden stamps on it in all beautiful rainbow colours, and we would count the stamps before Oliver climbed into bed hugging Pink Panther, and I would sing a Danish lullaby called '*Den lille Ole med para-blyen*', 'Little Ole with the Umbrella'.

I had a light breakfast and got ready for the big day. I put on my long purple cotton dress which had white flowers sewn onto it. I had put flowers around the brim of my old felt hat.

My dear friend Annie and I drove to the place where the wedding was set in a beautiful old barn built in the grounds of an old castle called Knebworth House. It is the home of Victorian novelist Edward Bulwer Lytton, who wrote 'It was a dark and stormy night,' and I had a vision at that moment in time driving towards the barn of Olivers dad playing his guitar in the nineties at Knebworth House, which is famous worldwide for its rock concerts.

When we walked into the barn, I looked at Oliver who was standing in the doorway and the sunlight was shining on his beautiful black hair. He was wearing a black three-piece tail-coat suit, and tears started to roll down my cheeks. . . how could it be that time had passed so quickly and he had become an adult and was getting married to a beautiful woman? Charlotte looked like a princess in her white lace sleeveless mermaid gown, walking down the aisle with her arm wrapped around her dad's.

It was a very beautiful warm day, and after the gorgeous dinner, I became tearful again seeing them together as a married couple doing their first dance, and I fell into my dreams, seeing me and Phil doing the first dance at our wedding in 1977 in a beautiful old cottage back in Denmark, not knowing that seven years later, Oliver would be born, and his beautiful brother Charlie would follow nine years later.

The night ended with tears and emotions running high, as I had to say my goodbyes to both boys as I was flying back to the US the next day.

CHAPTER 59

Falling in Love

I arrived back in Denver on the evening of 29th of July and James came to pick me up at the airport. I realised how much I had missed him, even though it was only four days ago we had said goodbye in Athens, when I had told him that I had fallen in love with him. I hugged him tight, and I looked into his big brown eyes and it felt good to be with him. Over the next month we decided that I should move in with him at his house.

I felt like a teenager in love as I packed my stuff and filled up James's car. I had my big Buddha on the car floor between my legs and still wrapped around its neck was my green emerald necklace I had kept for the memory of buying it in Switzerland. Strangely, I found out many years later it is the birthstone for Taurus born in April.

My little beach hut painting and all my treasures of beloved things which always followed me packed down in my suitcases on my life's journey, were now moving out of Niwot into a new adventure of living with James, moving into his house in late August 2018 after our first encounter around the family table in the Twin Peaks restaurant on a full moon night in January 2018.

Earth Ship

We have now travelled to so many beautiful places here in the US over the two years we lived in our old house, driving to New Mexico and James showing me Santa Fe, and passing through Taos, the soul of the southwest, experiencing rich spiritual traditions and fine art. I loved it there and want to go back some day. We have experienced staying in my dear friend, Kenny Young's, earth ship up in the hills of Taos. We drove to The Arches National Park in Utah which was a mind-blowing place. They call it 'Red Rock Wonderland' and I fell in love with these stunningly beautiful red rocks with their massive arches, feeling like a little matchstick standing underneath them. . . such an emotional experience to be there, as it was overpowering to me how nature in the US has become such a beautiful landscape on this earth.

We have also travelled to The Great Sand Dunes, thirty square miles of sand in North America. It has a dune tower 750 feet high. The experience of walking in the sand hand in hand was mind-blowing as it felt like we were in the middle of the Sahara Desert. I have taken James to see my second home in Barbados after years of travelling there, which was a beautiful time for me to show him a little of my past life.

Bouquet of Wildflowers

On a very warm spring day in March 2019, we decided to get married. We called my two boys back in England to celebrate with them on camera in our house. I had put on my beautiful Jonny Was long silk dress and let my hair hang over my shoulders. I put on my old faded rusty green felt hat with the bird feathers around the brim, which have been with me on my journey through my travels forever. I had bare feet and wore my silver ankle bracelet with little bells on it, and they made this beautiful church bells sound which reminded me of the trip we had taken to Santa Fe where James bought me the ankle bracelet. I had made a bouquet of wildflowers to hold in my hands, and James was wearing his blue faded jeans and a white shirt which clung to his chest, and he wore his turquoise desert boots he bought on our travels to England.

I fell back into my dreams of how we met in the restaurant one year before, falling in love through that year, and here we were, getting married. Entwined in each other's arms we raised our glasses with a beautiful red Château Musar wine, and we kissed in front of my boys on camera. I blew a kiss to my boys, and it felt so lovely that James was now a part of me and the boys.

We are now on a journey living together into our third year. We moved to our new house a year ago and we are weaving our lives like a plaited newly baked loaf, filled with love for each other. The butterflies which covered my body in the past have now been set free, flying away into the forever blue sky. .

.

James put The Kinks' song 'Set me Free' on the old record player, and we fell into each other's arms, gliding across the floor, dancing and sharing loving memories we both have of the past: James playing that song with his band 'The Rave', and me being a part of the Palmer and the Davies families, feeling the freedom we have given each other while we are surrounded by music, as James has started to play his guitar again after many moons passing. Stardust and angel wings were falling around us, and I let go of James's arms, still dancing in the clouds to the song 'Set me Free' as I slid into my studio, the sanctuary I have made for myself.

I see magical letters in all colours, flying around on their little wings, waiting to be made into stories, and my photography of magic moments I have experienced through my travels falling onto pages in a book wrapped in red ribbons and a little magical stardust falling on each page. I reach out with open arms, catching the sparkling letters one by one and sharing them with you readers in the moonlight of my written memoir of my life's journey of magic, fantasy, imagination, happiness, sadness, synchronicity, reality, and travelling the world, which are now so entwined in my soul and spirit. I have now let go of all inhibitions and opened my heart to you, to tell you my story.

Thank you for being with me on this magical mystery tour.

THE END

Acknowledgments

I would like to thank my beautiful soul sister Eva Andrea who inspired me to finish this memoir. Eva has not only been my mentor but has given me support and heartfelt love throughout. She has helped me to make my book a magical journey for the readers to enjoy.

I would also like to thank the very talented Annika Sylte for having the patience to create a perfect illustration of my eyes. She fulfilled my wish beautifully as seen on the front cover of this book.

I also want to thank Kim Macleod for guiding me through all the preparations required for the presentation of this book. It has come to life through the direction of Kim and Indie Authors World.

Most of all I like to thank my loving husband James being so patient with me writing my memoir in my little Sanctuary where it all came to life on paper. He has supported me in all kinds of ways with his passion for my book and his love hugs and kisses, and his beautiful mind helped me to make this book possible for your readers to read.

I would also like to thank the many friends, family, and the celebrities from all over the world for allowing me to share a small piece of their stories as presented in my book as well.

This memoir is purely written Through My Eyes from my own mind, memory and imagination as I have wandered through my journey in life.

Printed in Great Britain
by Amazon